HER STORY

WOMEN IN CHRISTIAN TRADITION

BARBARA J. MacHAFFIE

FORTRESS PRESS   PHILADELPHIA

To
Fraser Glen MacHaffie
Beverly Ann Zink
Ruth Patterson

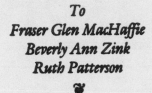

Fifth printing 1989

Library of Congress Cataloging-in-Publication Data

MacHaffie, Barbara J., 1949–
    Her story.

    Bibliography: p.
    Includes index.
    1. Women in Christianity—History. 2. Women in Christianity—United States—History. I. Title.
    BV639.W7M24   1986   270'. 088042   85-45494
    ISBN 0–8006–1893–9

4047E89   Printed in the United States of America   1–1893

CONTENTS

ACKNOWLEDGMENTS

The Program Agency of the Presbyterian Church (U.S.A.) and the Council on Women and the Church initiated this project. It has also been supported by Forest Hill Presbyterian Church, Cleveland Heights, Ohio, where I gave a series of popular lectures on this subject. Dr. Dieter Hessel of the Program Agency, P.C.U.S.A., and Thelma Megill-Cobbler of Fortress Press have been helpful editors and deserve my gratitude. Thanks are due to Mrs. Phyllis Zoerkler on the library staff at Marietta College for her assistance. Dr. Martin E. Marty, Dr. Robert Handy, Dr. Freda Gardner, Dr. Elizabeth Verdesi, Dr. Katie Cannon, and Professor Carolyn DeSwarte Gifford read the manuscript and greatly improved it with their suggestions. Dr. Bert Glaze of the Department of Economics, Management, and Accounting at Marietta College was kind enough to provide computer facilities for the preparation of the manuscript. The three people to whom this book is dedicated have given me resources for my work in more ways than I can ever describe or repay. I am particularly grateful to my husband Fraser for being a good listener and friend in a most uncommon union.

INTRODUCTION

Books surveying the history of Christianity have been traditionally "his stories" describing the flaws and celebrating the achievements of great theologians, eloquent preachers, and powerful administrators. This survey makes one contribution toward redressing the balance by illuminating in broad terms the forgotten history of over half of the Christian community. It represents "her story" not in the sense that women are treated in isolation from Western society and culture as a whole but in the sense that the focus is the status of women in the Christian tradition. The chapters cover the period from biblical times to the present day by asking questions such as: What roles did women play in leadership structures and in religious ceremonies? What roles did they find for themselves outside "official" institutional churches or the formalities of worship? How were females (persons who carry out the biological functions of women) and the feminine (characteristics assigned by cultural traditions to women) regarded in devotional and theological writing?

In the past twenty years, there has been an explosion in scholarship exploring the relationship between women and religion which has provided both the occasion for this particular survey as well as the shape of its contents. *Her Story* was motivated in part by a recognition that pastors, lay women and men, and college and seminary students would benefit from a study that draws together and reflects upon the fruits of current scholarship. That scholarship has in turn determined the contours of this book, and for this reason, it is worth exploring in more detail the way in which the study of women and the Christian past has developed. Kathryn Kish Sklar outlines several stages in the history of scholarship on women and American religion which can be applied to the study of women and Christianity in general and which converge in this text.[1]

1

Historians were at first concerned with gathering facts about the activities of women in Christian history both as individuals and as a group. They tried to make known what had previously been unknown or ignored. In a significant way, I have depended upon detailed investigation of historical data. The reader will learn, for example, that women once held quasi-episcopal status in medieval Europe, that they were preachers in early Methodism, and that they wrote commentaries on the Bible at the end of the nineteenth century.

Contemporary feminism, however, has brought a new approach to the study of the past. The approach, which I have adopted, frankly recognizes that the Christian tradition is intertwined with patriarchy and, on many occasions and in many places, functioned to oppress and degrade women. I have started from the assumption that the dignity, equality, and full participation of women in the Christian community are important. A critical exploration of church history shows that the achievement of these goals has been impeded, for example, by the words of the church fathers and the Victorian cult of true womanhood.

One response to the results of feminist scholarship has been to discard the Christian past as hopelessly oppressive. Another has been to move on in historical investigation to ask the question Have women ever benefited from the Christian tradition and have they actively contributed to it?[2] I have drawn on a wide range of scholarship that pursues these questions and answers affirmatively. I agree with Eleanor McLaughlin in her statement that "Christian faith and institutions have been at certain times and under certain conditions radically supportive of women and informed by women's experience."[3] The writings of the medieval mystics, the experiences of Perpetua, Katherine Zell, and Mary Webb and the influence of women's missionary efforts all belie the image of the Christian woman as passive and powerless. The support and meaning women found in the voluntary associations of the last century contradict the image of Christianity as consistently at odds with the interests and concerns of women.

The process of investigation in this third strand of historical study leads us in some unexpected directions. It takes us outside the culturally dominant Catholic and Protestant groups to movements such as Shakerism and Gnosticism. It also forces us to consider the personal expressions of faith found in letters, diaries, and devotional writings as well as the better-known theological works and sermons on which Christian history has come to depend. It also makes us aware of the need to push further into an exploration of the religious experience of women and to explore this experience in terms of a woman's racial, ethnic, and socioeconomic background.

hatred of women

There are a number of important questions that should be considered as one reads through the chapters of this study. What, for example, is the true source of misogyny in Western culture, with which the church is so often infused? Why do new movements in the tradition frequently give a wider role and higher status to women only to retreat as the group becomes established? Why is there so little theological writing by women? Were they simply not interested in analytical and rational reflection on God, or were their works deliberately neglected and suppressed? Were women silently protesting against their status in the mainstream churches when they joined groups that deviated from the culturally dominant traditions?

Answers to these questions may begin to take shape only after a much longer period of historical study in which the tools of other disciplines such as psychology and anthropology are used. What can be said with certainty is that the careful accumulation of historical data and clear principles for its reinterpretation will yield a usable past for women.

It is my conviction that women who undertake this venture will find a usable past. What is there to be discovered will dispel stereotypes, illumine current issues in the Christian community, and build up the sense of self-worth of women.

CHAPTER I

BIBLICAL IMAGES OF WOMEN

Many people who are concerned with the dignity and rights of women have abandoned the Christian tradition in despair. They point out that the Bible, the cornerstone of that tradition, was born and bred in cultures that treated women and the feminine as inferior and unworthy. They show us incidents in the pages of the Bible in which women are maimed, raped, and murdered, and explicitly regarded as the possessions of men. They cringe at arguments that have been voiced in second-century North Africa, seventeenth-century New England, and twentieth-century America—arguments like the following: The Old Testament tells us that woman was made after man in the natural order of creation. The Bible tells us that woman was responsible for bringing sin into the world. The New Testament clearly shows that Jesus chose men as his apostles to continue his work. Scripture explicitly prohibits women from exercising authority in the church and in the home and commands that they keep silent in the public assembly of God's people.

CRITICAL PRINCIPLES

There is, however, another approach to the biblical texts which takes seriously contemporary concerns to further the rights and interests of women. Many exponents also maintain that the Bible contains the authoritative word of God to humanity. This approach provides a new perspective on the biblical material coming to the tasks of translation and interpretation from a concern for the humanity and equality of women. This new departure in biblical studies involves several principles of interpretation.

1. *The Bible has been written, translated, and interpreted for centuries by men in cultures that were patriarchal.* In patriarchy, women are subordinated within the gradations of a hierarchical society. Material on women,

5

therefore, has often been misinterpreted or overlooked. In some instances, generic nouns and pronouns in the original languages have been translated into English as masculine words.

2. *A careful textual study must be made using all the available tools of biblical scholarship.* An accurate understanding of the meaning of words must be sought. Also, readers must try to discern the intentions of the author and try to gain a knowledge of the historical and social background of the biblical material.

3. *The Bible contains a great deal of material that treats women as subordinate and inferior to men. At the same time, there is a built-in judgment or critique of the degradation of women running through the Old and New Testaments which challenges the commands of silence and subordination.*

4. *The demands of God must be distinguished from the demands of a particular culture.* The Bible as a whole makes it clear that God's people are to bring justice and wholeness to all human beings. The injunctions that degrade women do not provide principles valid for every age of Christianity but instead reflect cultural situations in which men related to women through dominance. The standard for the Christian community today should be the glimmers of female dignity and leadership that shine through the pages of the Bible.

5. *The early church gives us only a preliminary hint at the new reality of the gospel.* It does not provide us with an ideal set of practices which we must slavishly follow but a dynamic set of beliefs about God's dealings with the human situation.

STATUS OF WOMEN IN HEBREW SOCIETY

The ancient Hebrews shared much in common with neighboring societies of the Near East. The social milieu reflected in the Old Testament is patriarchal, a word which literally means "father-rule." Men or the masculine were favored in every aspect of life. Religious, political, and military power was in the hands of men, who also controlled the sources of wealth. Evidence for this can be found in the legal and historical writings of the Old Testament. Although it is difficult to know with any certainty how often a law was enforced or how representative of women in general were the experiences of a particular woman in the narrative, it is possible to develop an overall picture of the status of women in Hebrew society.[1]

The Culture of the Covenant

Woman's Place. Only men were full-fledged members of the covenant community and the rite of circumcision made this explicit. As full members, they shared the privileges and responsibilities of social and religious life in ancient Israel. This situation is clear in the historical material which is primarily about men, although women do play a part occasionally and sometimes even steal the spotlight. In addition, the assumption underlying the laws of Israel is that they will be enforced and carried out by men.

Women at every stage in life clearly occupied a dependent and subordinate position. A woman began life under the rule of her father. Both the story of Jephthah's daughter (Judges 11:29–40) and that of Lot's daughters (Gen. 19:4–8) illustrate the extent to which the authority of a father could go. At the time of her marriage, a woman passed from the authority of her father to that of her husband. Women referred to their husbands as "ba'al" or "master," and they in turn were referred to as the property or possession of their husbands. There is no doubt that they were regarded as occupying a dependent, childlike position in the family.

Motherhood. A woman in ancient Israel was expected to marry and bear children. Her duties were primarily reproduction and nurturing, aimed at building up the household of her husband. In the historical writings the ideal wife is certainly portrayed as intelligent and resourceful, but she is always deferential to the well-being and desires of her husband. Her fulfillment was found in serving her husband and particularly in supplying him with many sons.

The image of woman as mother is a dominant one in the writings of the ancient Hebrews. Mothers are described as figures of compassion who jealously guard their children and who weep inconsolably over the death of their offspring. It is in the role of mother almost exclusively that the Hebrew woman is given respect and honor in society. The role of mother, however, also brought to a woman an opportunity to exercise a degree of power and authority over the household. The Old Testament contains examples of mothers who dedicate a child to the service of God (1 Sam. 1:11), attempt to influence the choice of a son's wife (Gen. 27:46—28:2), and try to have a favorite son declared the principal heir to his father's estate (Gen. 21:10). Never losing her dependent status, however, a woman had to turn to her sons for food and shelter if she was widowed. Barrenness was a dreaded curse because it deprived women of economic benefits and also because it removed an important source of authority and respect.

Sexuality. Although most of the Hebrew laws are aimed at the covenant community of men, there are certain laws that specifically concern women. These generally fall into two categories: laws concerning matters of marriage and sexuality, and laws concerning the religious life of women. In the first category, a double standard for men and women is clearly operating. Women, for example, were required to be virgins when they married, while men were not. A man could "dispossess" or divorce a wife but she could not divorce him. The prostitute was a figure of disrepute and shame, yet her services were enjoyed and sanctioned in every period of Hebrew history. Adultery did impose the identical penalty of death on both men and women. Yet even here it has been suggested that since only the female offender could become pregnant, she would be caught and punished many more times than her male partner. Also, a man could submit his wife to a humiliating and frightening ordeal (Num. 5:14–28) if he merely suspected her of unfaithfulness. She did not have a similar right. Finally, adultery was viewed as an offense against a husband by a deceitful wife. If a woman's husband engaged in sexual relations with a single woman outside of marriage, there was no penalty.

Worship. The legislative material dealing specifically with the worship of Yahweh (the Israelite name for God) also reveals the patriarchal society of ancient Israel. The priesthood, for example, was restricted to men. Women were permitted to participate in religious observances but with notable restrictions. In keeping with the laws of ritual purity, women who were menstruating or who had recently given birth were considered to be unclean for specified periods of time (Lev. 12:1–5; 15:19–30). For women of child-bearing age, this certainly impaired their ability to participate in religious rituals. These laws became increasingly restrictive after the Jews returned from Babylon. They attempted to prevent a similar calamity by insisting on a strict observance of the laws of ritual purity. The participation of women was limited, finally, by the provision of Deut. 16:16, which exempted them from attending the three annual pilgrim feasts, focal points of Hebrew religious life. Gradually, some of the activities women were not required to do became activities they were not allowed to do.

Israel in Dispersion

The Jews in the centuries before the birth of Jesus were dispersed throughout the ancient Near East. Religious life was carried on in the synagogues under rabbis who taught the contents of the Law and the Prophets, applying them to daily life. Differing locations and cultures produced some variations in the status of Jewish women. It appears that some communities, influenced by Greek and Roman culture, began to allow women more freedom in social and religious life. There is evidence that women became leaders of synagogues in a few places and there are indications that on occasion, women divorced their husbands. Generally, however, the patriarchal pattern continued and even became more rigid in the teachings of the rabbis.

The rabbinic literature regards women as socially and religiously inferior to men and sometimes even expresses contempt for them. Men were cautioned against speaking to women in public. It was feared that a female voice would seduce a man and lead to corruption. Women were not permitted to be witnesses in a court of law, nor were they counted in the quorum necessary for the formation of a synagogue congregation. At the temple in Jerusalem they were restricted to an outer court. In the synagogues they were seated separately and were not permitted to read aloud or to assume any public position. Perhaps most significantly, they were not permitted to study the Scriptures. One first-century rabbi vigorously made this point when he wrote, "Rather should the words of the Torah be burned than to be entrusted to a woman. . . . " One widely used rabbinic prayer declared, "Praised be God that he has not created me a gentile; praised be God that he has not created me a woman; praised be God that he has not created me an ignorant man."[2]

THE OLD TESTAMENT CRITIQUE OF PATRIARCHY

Exceptional Hebrew Women

One important aspect of biblical studies responsive to the concerns of women has been the rediscovery of exceptional women in the Old Testament. These are women who in some way challenged the subordinate status assigned to them in Hebrew culture. Striking examples of outstanding women are the four who are called "prophets" or ones through whom God spoke. Miriam (Exod. 15:20–21), Deborah (Judges 4:4–6), and Huldah (2 Kings 22:14–20) are all regarded as authoritative channels for divine truth. Noadiah (Neh. 6:14) is referred to as a false prophet, but in none of these instances is any special attention given to the fact that the prophets are women. It is true that no identifiable writings from female prophets survive, probably because they were not associated with groups of disciples who could preserve their oracles. Also, women prophets exercised their gifts alongside of their responsibilities as wives and mothers. Nevertheless, they clearly illustrate the Hebrew belief that God could communicate messages of vital importance through either men or women.

A number of other women who showed independent judgment and exercised significant influence are revealed in a careful examination of the Old Testament books. We can only mention a few of them. Athaliah ruled as queen over Judah from 842 until 837 B.C. Her methods were ruthless and her devotion was to Ba'al rather than Yahweh but she, like Jezebel, showed initiative, boldness, and independence. Queen Alexandra reigned over a peaceful and prosperous Judah several centuries later (78 –69 B.C.). Second Samuel describes two incidents in which women, noted for their wisdom, were consulted at critical times in the political and military history of Israel (2 Sam. 14:1–20 and 2 Sam. 20:14–22). The child Moses is saved by the cooperation of his mother and sister with the women of the royal household of Egypt (Exod. 2:1–10).

The stories of Vashti, Esther, and Ruth have received significant reinterpretation in light of contemporary concern over the status of women in church and society. Vashti in later Judeo-Christian tradition was reviled for her disobedience to her husband (Esther 1:10–12), yet she shows remarkable courage for her refusal to debase herself before a group of drunken men. Esther, on the other hand, is celebrated for using her beauty and deferential behavior as a model wife to save the Jewish people. We are encouraged to note in both stories that women took risks for their convictions, not that some women disobeyed their husbands while others did not. Ruth, like Esther, is often used as an appropriate role model for women, yet it is important to focus less on her deference to Boaz and more on the ways in which she actually shaped her own destiny and made radical choices that defied custom. In this important story, "one female has chosen another female in a world where life depends upon men. There is no more radical decision in all the memories of Israel."[3] The story of Ruth, along with earlier figures such as Tamar (Genesis 38), help us rediscover the crucial and controversial role of women as keepers of the covenant.

Feminine and Female Imagery for
God in the Old Testament

Although the Hebrews believed that God was beyond all human definitions and limitations, including sexuality, they continued to use terms to describe Yahweh that made sense in their particular cultural context. Since this culture was patriarchal, masculine and male images for God are plentiful throughout the Old Testament. God is described as king, warrior, father, shepherd, and jealous husband. Yet these images are complemented by a number of feminine and female descriptions, which have been ignored. These images may have been encouraged by the lingering tendency of the Hebrews to worship a goddess as well as Yahweh.[4] Whatever their origins, they are far more evident than is often realized.

God as Mother. The strongest female image for God is that of mother. In a conversation between God and Moses, for example, Moses depicts God in the images of mother and wetnurse (Num. 11:12). In some versions of

Deuteronomy, the people of Israel are accused of forgetting "the Rock who bore you" and the God who "gave you birth" (Deut. 32:18). The prophetic material is an even richer source of feminine and female imagery. Hosea not only uses the image of Yahweh as the husband of fatherless Israel, but he describes Yahweh as performing the many tasks that a mother performed in Hebrew society—feeding a child, teaching it to walk, healing its injuries (Hos. 11:1, 3–4). The prophet of the exile, whose writings are included in the Book of Isaiah, refers to God as the one who has carried Israel "from the womb" (Isa. 46:3–4) and who cries out like a woman in labor (Isa. 42:14). In the context of an entire passage celebrating the female as a source of strength and life (Jer. 31:22), Jeremiah speaks of the God who displays "motherly compassion" in some translations of the Hebrew.

Divine Wisdom as Female. When the people of Israel returned to their homeland after the Babylonian exile, they made great efforts to protect themselves from foreign influence and the goddess worship that often implied. The feminine and female imagery for God found in the earlier material now becomes less direct but by no means disappears. Such tendencies are channeled into the feminine figure of Wisdom, which appears in the Book of Proverbs and in Job 28. Wisdom is feminine not only grammatically (in both the Hebrew and Greek languages) but Wisdom is also described as a "lady," "mistress," and "sister." Wisdom in Proverbs is an aspect or part of God that was with God at the beginning of creation (Prov. 8:22–31) and a source of delight and good advice to God (Prov. 8:12–21). Wisdom is the feminine side of God which can be known by human beings and which is to be sought after (Prov. 4:5–9, 11–13). She extends happiness to those who find her (Prov. 3:13–18).

A New Look at the Creation Stories of Genesis

There are two accounts of the creation of humanity in Genesis. Scholars are generally agreed that the story in Genesis 2—3 is the older of the two and was probably composed by editors who wrote in the tenth century B.C. The account in Genesis 1 probably comes from the hands of an editor (or editors) who lived several centuries later. Both of these accounts have been given new attention and Genesis 2—3 has received fresh interpretation.[5]

It has often been argued in the churches that women must be subordinate to men because woman was created after man in the order of creation. Yet each story in Genesis teaches that men and women were created as equals. In Gen. 1:26 the RSV translation, "Let us make man in our own image . . . " is more correctly translated as, "Let us make humanity in our own image. . . . " Verse 27 goes on to say that male and female were created simultaneously, not one after the other. There is no subordination here, only differentiation. Over the past century women have observed also that the image of God in which humanity is made contains both male and female characteristics.

Genesis 2 is often quoted to reinforce the subordination of women to men. Here we find woman created after man, out of his rib and as his helpmate. A careful look at the structure and language of the story, however, radically alters the traditional understanding.

The first episode of the account (2:7–24) opens with the creation of *'ādām*, which Phyllis Trible argues persuasively should be translated as "earth creature." In these early verses, *'ādām* should be understood as a human being without sexual differences.[6] The story goes on to tell that the earth creature was lonely, so Yahweh sought a suitable companion. When the animals proved unsuitable, Yahweh created another earth creature and introduced sexual differences, thus bringing male and female (*ish* and *ishah*) into being simultaneously. After this point in the story, *'ādām* can be translated accurately as "male creature." The author, however, builds ambiguity into the term. The episode moves from wholeness to differentiation but then back to wholeness again as the two become one flesh.

The Hebrew word *'ēzer* which is translated "helper" (v. 18) does not imply that the woman was in any way inferior to the man or the human creature. The word simply describes a beneficial relationship between two parties in which one helps the other. God, for example, is frequently referred to as the helper of Israel. There is no sense in which the helper is subordinate to the one in need.

Also the fact that woman comes from the rib of the man or the creature does not mean that she is inferior. God alone performs the creative act while the man or creature is asleep. God uses the material of the rib to build woman just as the earth was used initially. Woman is no more subordinate to man or the creature than man or the creature is to the earth used in the creative process.

Even if the second Genesis story does not authorize the subordination of women in its description of the original creation, there have been many attempts to impose that subordination on the grounds that the first woman brought sin and death into the world. A favorite argument of theologians throughout Christian history has been that God sentenced woman to be subject to her husband and to bear children in pain as a penalty for her disobedience. In the words of the early Christian theologian Tertullian, "*You* are the Devil's gateway: *you* are the unsealer of that forbidden tree: you are the first deserter of divine law: you are she who per-

suaded him who the devil was not valiant enough to attack. *You* destroyed
so easily God's image, man."[7]

There are alternative ways, however, of interpreting this story. The account tells us that the man and woman are both present when the serpent
approaches. It is interesting to speculate why the woman is chosen as a
partner for conversation. It may be because the woman was traditionally
associated with the preparation of food, or it may be because the woman
appeared to be imaginative and thoughtful. The woman is certainly portrayed by the writer as intelligent and aware of what the forbidden tree had
to offer. She is also sensitive to the beauty of the tree and the goodness of
the food it provided. She acts independently and takes the initiative. She is
perceptive enough to know that the command from God not to eat from
the tree applied to her even though it was given before she was created.
While the man simply gobbles up the fruit that is offered to him, she
struggles with a theological issue—the temptation to disobey. Nowhere
in the story is the woman accused of seducing the male. Rather, the verb
"to seduce" or "to deceive" is used only in connection with the serpent's
activities. Nowhere does the story say that the woman tempted the man or
used wicked persuasion. The text simply says, "She gave some to her husband and he ate" (Gen. 3:6b).

The judgments passed on the couple as a result of their disobedience can
also be given a new interpretation. What we find in Gen. 3:14–19 is a description of life as it is lived in disobedience to God. In the story, the su-
premacy of male over female is condemned as a perversion of creation.
God intended male and female to be equals in the created order. This is a
remarkable assertion for a writer steeped in patriarchal culture. It raises the
question of how men and women are to relate in the community of grace
where sin has been forgiven.

A New Look at the Song of Solomon

Women in Hebrew culture acted as creators and transmitters of stories,
poems, and ballads, which related important events in the history of the
people. The songs of Deborah and Miriam are two good examples of this
function (Judges 5; Exod. 15:21). Another less noted literary expression
that may come from the pen of a woman or a group of women is the Song
of Songs or Solomon. The book was probably written in the third century
B.C. although it seems to include material of an earlier date. It is a poetic
description of the love between a man and a woman. It may be in the Old
Testament because it reminded the people of Israel of the love God had
shown to them. Whatever its origins, the Song of Solomon reflects an understanding of women that challenges the patriarchal view.[8]

Women dominate this series of love poems. The female partner in the love relationship opens the composition in chapter 1 and closes it in chapter 8. The woman has most of the dialogue in the book—eighty-four verses—while her lover speaks in only forty-nine verses. A group of women referred to as the "daughters of Jerusalem" are appealed to for support in several places. The mothers both of the woman and her partner are important figures in the composition.

Even more significant is the relationship described here between the woman and the man. The relationship is one of mutuality and equality rather than subordination and dependence (2:16). The woman keeps vineyards and looks after flocks (1:6, 8), tasks the man also assumes. At times her lover approaches her, and at other times she initiates their lovemaking (3:1–4). She describes the beauty of the male just as he describes her beauty. Their relationship is one of tenderness and respect. They celebrate the joys of sexual attraction and love. Perhaps most significantly, the woman is valued in the poem for more than her reproductive abilities. There is no mention made of her role as mother, so important in Hebrew culture.

The Song of Solomon can also be interpreted as providing a thought-provoking commentary on the story in Genesis 2—3. Both the poem and the Genesis story use the image of a beautiful garden filled with animals as well as trees which are lovely to look at and good for food. What we have in the Song of Solomon, however, is a description of male-female relationships as God intended them to be and not as they exist in a disobedient world. The paradise that was lost in Eden has been regained in the garden of this poem. The man and woman are not ashamed of their nakedness, the man desires the woman and she desires him, and they live in a situation in which there is no male dominance or female subordination.

THE NEW TESTAMENT PICTURE

Since the members of the Christian community claim to be followers of Jesus in some way, it is logical that the scriptural accounts of the attitudes of Jesus toward women should play a major part in shaping their views. The writers of the four Gospels have provided Christians with the memory of the life and teachings of Jesus. In studying these books, it is important to remember that the Gospel writers are not trying to give us a completely objective, accurate, and detailed account of Jesus' work on earth. Rather, they are using stories and teachings in a selective way to make a statement about the meaning of Jesus' life for men and women. They include much of themselves and the prejudices of their culture in their writing. It is as though we are seeing Jesus through the lens of these early Christians.

The cultural context in which the first Christians lived and wrote tended to devalue women and the feminine. Yet in the early church's portrayal of Jesus, this perspective is never conveyed. Jesus never treats women as inferior to men. His words are filled with positive images of women and he defends their equality and full humanity many times in his ministry.[9] The fact that this impression has been transmitted through the writings of men who shared the assumptions of their culture indicates how strong this feature was in the ministry of Jesus.

Women Disciples

Women were clearly counted as among those who were taught by and who traveled with Jesus as "disciples." This fact alone suggests his positive attitude toward women. All three Synoptic Gospels (Mark 15:40–41; Luke 8:1–3; Matt. 27:55–56) describe both specific women and a general group of women as followers of Jesus. These women broke with Jewish custom in order to leave their homes and travel openly with Jesus. Jesus also contradicted accepted notions of woman's place by condoning and encouraging his female followers. The Gospel of John also supports the idea that women were intimate disciples of Jesus.[10] In the parable of the Good Shepherd (10:3–5) John compares the disciples of Jesus to sheep who know the shepherd's voice when he calls them by name. Mary Magdalene, so often referred to as a follower of Jesus, conforms to this description when she recognizes the voice of the risen Jesus as he calls her "Mary" (20:16).

The teaching of women by Jesus is particularly significant when we consider the customs of Judaism in his time. Women, as we noticed earlier in this chapter, were not permitted to study the Scriptures with a rabbi. Along with these general references to women disciples who were taught by Jesus, the story of Mary and Martha (Luke 10:38–42) clearly shows Jesus' willingness to consider women as worthy students. In the text, Mary takes the traditional male role of "sitting at the feet" or studying with the rabbi. Jesus approves of her interest in intellectual and spiritual matters, for she is told that she has chosen "the better part." Women are seen here as being capable of more than domestic service and hospitality.

Stories of Jesus

According to the Gospel writers, the content and style of the teachings of Jesus also reflect an untraditional view of women. The stories he told and the brief sayings he used to make a particular point often contain images appealing to men and women. Jesus addressed both men and women, inviting all to hear and respond to his words. An example of sexual pairing in the sayings of Jesus is found in Matt. 24:40–41 where it is not gender but faith that makes the decisive difference on the day of God's judgment.

Another pair of stories occurs in Luke, where Jesus is discussing the necessity for perseverance in prayer. One story involves a man who goes to his friend in the middle of the night to ask for bread (11:5–9). A story very similar in message and structure appears several chapters later with a widow as the main character (18:1–8). In telling stories that teach both men and women, Jesus even does not hesitate to use a feminine image to describe God. In Luke 15 Jesus uses the image of shepherd and father to emphasize God's concern for those who are lost. He also compares God to a woman who seeks diligently for a lost coin. His audience in this instance was made up of scribes and Pharisees, religious men who insisted on the strict subordination of women according to the Law.

The acts of ministry that are retold in the Gospels about Jesus provide an additional dimension to his spoken concern for the equality and full humanity of women. The Gospels contain many examples of this attitude, but it is especially evident in the stories of the woman with an issue of blood and of the Samaritan woman at the well. Matthew (9:18–26), Mark (5:24–34), and Luke (8:40–56) all record the story of a woman who had suffered for twelve years with a flow of blood, perhaps menstrual. Because of the ancient laws regarding cleanliness, she was excluded from participating in any religious rituals. Also, the objects and people she touched were made unclean. Jesus, however, did not shrink from her touch. He not only rejected the idea that such a woman was displeasing in the eyes of a holy God, but he used the opportunity to make those around him aware of his untraditional views.

In the story of the Samaritan woman, which is only found in the Gospel of John (4:1–42), Jesus also violates the traditional code governing the relationships between men and women. Not only does he, a Jew, speak to a Samaritan, but he disregards the Jewish norm prohibiting men from speaking to women in public. Rabbis especially were expected to obey such a rule. Jesus instead initiates a conversation with this woman as she comes to draw water from the well. Furthermore, he is willing to take a drink from her despite the Jewish belief that all Samaritan women were unclean (that is, menstruants) from birth. The Gospel writer continues to tell us that it is to this woman that Jesus first revealed himself as the Messiah. He sends her back to her village with this message, and her words cause many others to believe in Jesus. Here a woman is sent by Jesus to preach the good news of the gospel. John describes both the work of the male disciples and the vital witness of women in bringing people to Jesus. Later, at the raising of Lazarus, a woman, Martha, confesses that Jesus is the Christ (John 11:17–27).

The teachings of Jesus and his acts of ministry frequently focus on life situations that are of particular concern to women. In a number of passages, for example, he shows compassion for the widow who has been robbed of her status as wife and who has virtually no means of livelihood. Jesus recognizes clearly the plight of the widow in his stories such as those found in Luke 18:1–8 and Mark 12:41–44. He condemns the scribes for their oppression of the widow (Mark 12:38–40) and he raises to life the only son of the widow of Nain (Luke 7:11–17). Even in the midst of his agonizing death he provides for his mother's future by transferring to his "beloved disciple" his own responsibility for Mary's welfare (John 19:25–27).

Jesus' teaching on marriage and divorce also reflects, according to many scholars, his unique concern for the dignity of women. Mark 10:11–12, which is considered to be the text closest to the original words of Jesus, makes some unusual assertions. Jesus claims that the husband and wife have equal obligations in the marriage relationship. Divorce is condemned for both man and woman. No longer can a husband, using a male prerogative, discard his wife for either trivial or important reasons. Also, Jesus here acknowledges that a husband can commit adultery against his wife. In the culture of Jesus' day, only a wife could sin against her husband in adultery. A married man was free to engage in sexual relations with single women.

Women's Apostolate

Women have an important place in the teachings and ministry of Jesus, and this is confirmed in the Gospel accounts of the final days of his life. Women risk their physical well-being by openly weeping for him in the hostile crowd following Jesus to the place of his execution (Luke 23:26–32). In all the Gospels, women stay with Jesus through his crucifixion and in both Mark and Matthew their faithfulness is contrasted starkly with the behavior of his male disciples who "deserted him and ran away" (Matt. 26:56 and Mark 14:50). Their devotion to Jesus may have resulted from the compassion and dignity he gave to women in a culture that favored men.

A final example of Jesus' favor toward women and their loyalty to him can be found in the Gospel stories of the risen Jesus. All four accounts show a remarkable unanimity in their description of the discovery of the empty tomb: It was made by women who had come to mourn (Matt. 28:1; Mark 16:1–2; Luke 24:1–12; John 20:1–10). Also, Jesus appears first to a woman or women in the stories of Matthew, Mark, and John (Matt. 28:8–10; Mark 16:9–11; John 20:11–18). These accounts contradict Paul in 1 Cor. 15:5–8. It is important to note that in Mark and Matthew the angel of the Lord sends the women to tell the male disciples that Jesus has risen, and in Matthew and John, Jesus himself sends them on this mission. The cultural belief that women could not be trusted as witnesses to the truth is flouted by the risen Jesus. The women act for him as "apostles" or as ones who are sent to bear witness to the gospel.

A word must be said about the role of Mary Magdalene in the drama of Jesus' death and resurrection. Her name is included first on the lists of women described as being present at the crucifixion, burial, and empty tomb. A strong tradition that claimed that Jesus first appeared to Mary probably existed in the early churches. This belief is reflected in John's story of the resurrection. Some early Christian writings which were part of the dominant Catholic tradition gave Mary Magdalene a place of honor. She is described as an "apostle" in a biblical commentary from the second century and also in an account of her life written in the ninth century. Other written works, such as the *Pistis Sophia* and the *Gospel of Mary*, emerging from groups that deviated from the dominant Catholic tradition, place Mary in a position of significant leadership in the early church, even above the apostle Peter.

THE WRITINGS OF THE APOSTLE PAUL

Aside from the creation stories, the writings of the apostle Paul have been cited most frequently in discussions of the status of women in the Christian community. Paul has been condemned as the eternal enemy of women and celebrated as the only consistent spokesman for the liberation of women in the New Testament. Where does the truth lie? Probably somewhere in between.[11]

First, it must be pointed out that Paul is probably not the author of certain passages often cited in support of the view that he degraded women. It is likely that these passages (Col. 3:18; Eph. 5:21–33; Titus 2:3–5; 1 Tim. 2:8–15; 5:3–16; 1 Cor. 14:33b–36) originated at a later time and reflect changes in the environment of the early Christian community as well as in its organizational structure. They will be discussed in chapter 2.

The material that does come from Paul himself reflects an ambivalence toward women. He is a man in conflict. On the one hand, Paul knows the transforming power of the gospel and he clearly recognizes that relationships in the human community would be altered dramatically as a result. On the other hand, his own background as a Jew who strictly observed the law intrudes upon his belief that women and men are all full participants in the baptized community.

Galatians 3:28

Paul's recognition of the radical difference that life in Christ makes to people is summed up in Gal. 3:28. The Jewish male of Paul's day was expected to thank God daily that he was not a Gentile, a slave, or a woman. The man of Greek culture used a similar formula to express the same sentiments. Yet in the Christian community, these natural and social barriers break down. The values, roles, and customs of the world are replaced by a new reality. It is important to see that this new order of existence applied not only to a person's relationship with God but also to the actual life of the congregation. Paul claims that the conditions that would exist in the future kingdom of God are in some ways already realized in the community of believers.

The words of this verse probably do not originate with Paul but instead come from an early statement of faith affirmed by new converts to Christianity at the time of their baptism. They show that the equality of women reflected in Gal. 3:28 was part of the practice of the Christian community from its earliest days. Paul inherited this situation but he also gives his approval to it, not only by including these words in his Letter to the Galatians, but also by warmly greeting and commending women workers in the churches. In Phil. 4:2, for example, Paul explicitly states that Euodia and Syntyche have "contended" side by side with him as contestants would in an athletic competition. Several women are commended in Romans 16 for "laboring" with him in the Lord, and he readily sends greetings to women who led house churches (Philemon 2; 1 Cor. 16:19). There is no hint in these passages that Paul regarded the work of these women as in any way inferior to his own.

1 Corinthians 7:1–40

This section of Corinthians is a lengthy discussion on the subject of marriage. Clues in the text indicate that Paul was addressing himself to a group in the congregation that advocated celibacy, perhaps in imitation of Paul himself. There is considerable disagreement over the meaning of this passage for the status of women, but we can single out several important points Paul is making.

His comments on the marriage relationship are unusual in light of his own Jewish and Hellenistic background as well as the cultural situation in which he is writing. Marriage, as he describes it, shows a surprising degree of mutuality between husband and wife. There are six passages in 1 Corinthians 7 (vv. 3–4, 10–11, 12–13, 14, 16, 32–33) that suggest reciprocal or equal responsibilities in the relationship. He claims, for example, that "the wife does not rule over her own body but the husband does; likewise the husband does not rule over his own body but the wife does." This is a remarkable statement for a man writing in the first century.

In this passage Paul also plants a seed that has the effect of opening up a new social alternative for women. He presents celibacy as a way of living because he believes the end of time to be near. Women can choose not to marry and raise children. They are given a vocational status in which they are not only independent but accepted as equals by their male co-workers. In the future, Paul's ideas on the renunciation of marriage would be shaped by the church into a life style that was often liberating for women.

Despite these new departures in 1 Corinthians 7 Paul still adheres to the old pattern of female subjection in the home. Servitude, however, now applies to the male, to a certain extent, as well as the female. Marriage, like slavery, was a relationship of bondage in a scheme of things that would soon pass away. Neither of these institutions would become bearers of the dramatic new life of freedom in Christ, but would be eradicated at the end of time which Paul expected.

1 Corinthians 11:2–16

The ambivalent attitudes that Paul holds on the status of women become obvious in this passage from 1 Corinthians. In light of the restrictions placed on women in the synagogue and temple, it is astonishing that Paul even discusses appropriate dress for women who participate in public worship. He clearly assumes in verse 5 that women can be vehicles of God's spirit. They, like men, can pray and prophesy in the congregation, and by prophesying, Paul meant intelligible preaching that built up the faith of the church.

In this passage, however, Paul launches into a "bad-tempered tirade" in which his inbred attitudes toward the status of women take over.[12] This passage appears within a long section on the proper way to conduct worship. It seems that Paul was concerned with curbing the abuses and stopping the chaos in the Corinthian church. He had a vision of liberation which certainly included women, but he recoils from the social disorder that seemed to accompany the practical implementation of this freedom. He reacts by insisting that women cover their heads when praying or prophesying in the congregation.

In the process of defending his position, Paul explicitly argues for the subordination of women to men. The head covering was necessary because it symbolized the subjection of the female. God was the head of Christ, Christ the head of the male, and the male the head of the female. Paul turns to rabbinic Judaism to defend his position in verses 8 and 9. Woman was made from man and in his image, according to Genesis 2. Also, she was made *for* man, to exist as his helper. It is interesting that he does not use the argument of 1 Timothy which states that women are subordinate because they are morally inferior to men. He then supplements this theological defense with an appeal in verse 13 to what was proper or customary in his social setting.

Paul's comments in verse 10 and his discussion of hair styles in verses 14–15 are puzzling. He may be reflecting the beliefs of first-century Judaism in his claim that women should cover their heads "because of the angels." It was commonly believed that in the early days of the human race, women were seduced by fallen angels and gave birth to demons as a result of this union. This story, based on Gen. 6:1–4, appeared in later Jewish literature. According to its logic, women had to cover their heads in order to protect themselves against the onslaught of evil. The underlying assumption was that women are weak and easily influenced by demonic forces. It is possible that Paul is expressing his anxiety over whether or not women could remain steadfast in their faith.

Paul suddenly interrupts himself in verses 11 and 12 with a comment that seems to undermine his argument. He is unable to keep himself from making a qualifying remark, showing the deep impact that the transforming power of the gospel had on his upbringing. These verses express a degree of mutual support between male and female that is more compatible with Gal. 3:28. The general lines of Paul's argument in 1 Corinthians 11 follow the presuppositions of his culture, but by inserting these two verses, he points to a new set of assumptions operating in the body of Christ.

The conflicting attitudes toward women which Paul seems to demonstrate serve to highlight the tension present in the biblical material in general. On the one hand, patriarchy is evident throughout the history of Israel and resurges both in the rabbinic culture of first-century Judaism and in some of Paul's writings. On the other hand, there is a built-in critique of patriarchy running through the Old Testament as well as the ministry of Jesus.

Much of this chapter has focused on male attitudes toward women in the Christian community, leaving us with the question of what women were actually doing and thinking in the nascent Christian community. Possible answers to this question are suggested in the next chapter on women in the biblical and postbiblical churches.

CHAPTER 2

WOMEN AND
THE EARLY CHURCHES

WOMEN IN THE NEW TESTAMENT CHURCHES

The Prominence of Women

Anyone who wishes to study the status of women in the first six centuries of Christian history is faced with a challenging task. During this period the church spread beyond Judaism and Palestine into the vast expanse of Greco-Roman culture. It was both persecuted and elevated to a position of eminence, all the while struggling to come to terms with the intellectual movements of the ancient world. The variations in belief and practice from place to place and century to century are great. At the same time, our sources of information for this phase are scarce and often fragmentary and ambiguous. Yet the early years of Christianity are vital to the status of women, for they established attitudes and practices that still continue in the Christian community.

Recovering Lost Tradition. Biblical scholar and theologian Elisabeth Schüssler Fiorenza makes some important suggestions for those who want to explore the activities of women in the early church.[1] She reminds us that our sources of information, mainly the Book of Acts and the epistles of the New Testament along with scattered later material on church order, have been written and interpreted in patriarchal cultures with unfortunate results. We have overlooked, for example, the information in the New Testament on the work of women and instead assumed that the church was a "man's church." We have assumed also that the categories such as "apostle" and "prophet" only include men unless women are specifically mentioned. Instead, these terms, even when specifically masculine, should be read as inclusive until we have clear evidence to the contrary. She points out several instances where masculine terms are known to include women. Finally, she urges us to remember that what we know about the activities of women probably only represents the tip of the iceberg. It is likely that women participated in the early development of the church to a much greater extent than our sources imply.

We must not forget, first of all, that women were included as full members of the Christian communities. In light of the Jewish practice that defined a synagogue congregation by the number of circumcised males present, this inclusive membership was unusual. Saul, before his conversion, sets out to arrest both men and women who have adopted the new faith (Acts 8:3; 9:2). Acts 17:11–12 claims that in Beroea, a Macedonian city, both men and women "received the word with all eagerness, examining the Scriptures daily to see if these things were so." Also, Luke's Gospel contains evidence that it was shaped by a social context in which large numbers of women were interested in and responding to the Christian message.[2] Luke provides us with a rich source of material on Jesus' teachings about women and his ministry with them.

Women were clearly involved in the spread of Christianity and in the establishment of new congregations which met in private houses. Paul refers to women who have been his co-workers in the evangelization of the Hellenistic world. In Romans 16, he commends Mary, Tryphana, Tryphosa, and Persis for having "labored hard" in the Lord. In the same chapter, he pays tribute to the outstanding missionary work of Priscilla (or Prisca) and her husband Aquila. In Phil. 4:2, Euodia and Syntyche are described as women who have worked or "contended" side by side with Paul. There is no indication in these passages that women were subordinate to or dependent upon Paul.

The house churches were crucial to the success of the early mission efforts since they provided support and sustenance to the growing Christian congregations. They were the places in which the Lord's Supper was celebrated and the gospel preached. It is recorded that women provided the facilities for some groups, especially if they were wealthy and prominent members of the community. Acts 16:14, for example, mentions Lydia, a successful businesswoman, who offered her house to the Christian church. Although many interpreters of the New Testament in the past have translated the name in Col. 4:14 as the male name "Nymphas," it is generally agreed that the verse correctly reads, "Nympha who had a church in her house." The house of Mary, the mother of John Mark, was also used in this way (Acts 12:12).

Leadership Roles. The communal life of the early Christians acquired organizational structure very quickly. Every member, male and female, was regarded as having certain gifts from the Holy Spirit which could be used in the service of the community. It appears therefore that there was no "ministry" as distinct from the "laity." Some of these gifts were given to members who had been appointed in a formal way by the community to do a variety of tasks. Others were given directly and indiscriminately by the Holy Spirit and were simply recognized by the community.

The community selected certain members to occupy positions of authority and leadership. The earliest figures of authority were the apostles or those who had been commissioned by the risen Jesus to preach the gospel. They in turn appointed groups of elders (or presbyters) in the new congregations. They based this appointment on the organizational model of the Jewish synagogue. The elders probably exercised a variety of functions which eventually included teaching, discipline, the regulation of worship, and the pastoral care of the community. The president or leader of the council of elders gradually became identified as the bishop or "overseer" who was particularly responsible for the sacraments and the pastoral care of the congregation. The New Testament, however, seems to use the titles of presbyter and bishop interchangeably.

The question relevant to this particular study is whether or not women occupied any of these leadership roles. The direct evidence is limited but may only hint at what was actually happening. The New Testament does not refer directly to women as presbyters or bishops but it does indicate that women occupied influential positions of leadership in the churches.

In the New Testament women are not only described as the patronesses of house churches but also as their leaders. The letter to Philemon greets Apphia "our sister" who together with Philemon and Archippus was a leader of the house church at Colossae. Also, in 1 Thess. 5:12 Paul commands the church to give respect and recognition to the laborers and coworkers who are "over you in the Lord." In other places he uses these identical descriptive phrases to refer to his female colleagues. He believes that the authority of Euodia and Syntyche (Philippians 4), who worked with him at Philippi, was so great that their dissension would do serious damage to the community.

Phoebe appears to have been a prominent woman in the early church. Paul calls her both *diakonos* and a *prostasis* in Romans 16, titles which have been misinterpreted traditionally. *Diakonos*, although grammatically masculine, is usually translated as "deaconess," implying that Phoebe only did the subservient and female-oriented tasks of the deaconess in later Christian history. Yet when Paul uses this word in other contexts, he is referring to individuals who preach and teach as official congregational leaders. Also, *prostasis* is usually translated as "helper" or "patroness" but in the literature of the first century, the word commonly means a leader, president, or superintendent. It is probable that Phoebe not only held great authority in Cenchreae but was widely respected throughout the Christian community.

Romans 16:7 probably reveals another female leader of the early church. Here Andronicus and Junia are commended for their outstanding work in spreading the gospel. Again, translators in the past have found it inconceivable that a woman would be called "apostle" and so they use the male name "Junias." Junia, however, was a common female name in the first century. Also, the Gospel accounts of the risen Jesus reveal that women could fulfill the requirements for the role of apostle. They have a direct confrontation with the risen Jesus and they receive a commission from him to preach the gospel.

DEUTERO-PAULINE REACTION

A strong protest against the leadership of women in the early churches is registered in several passages of the New Testament (Col. 3:18; Eph. 5:21–33; Titus 2:3–5; 1 Tim. 2:8–15; 5:3–16; 1 Cor. 14:33b–36). These passages were probably written between A.D. 80 and 125. They do not describe the status of women in all the churches but instead try to impose upon the Christian communities the patriarchal standards of the ancient world. This approach eventually prevailed in the Christian churches but not without difficulty. Throughout the early centuries, church authorities continued to rule against the leadership of women, an indication that women persisted in assuming authoritative roles in some places.

The passages listed in the paragraph above have been distinguished from the earlier writings of Paul on the basis of several criteria.[3] The style and vocabulary are different from what appear to be the genuine works of the Apostle. Also, the outlook or perspective of these chapters differs from the material we considered in chapter 1. In some places, the verses probably have been inserted into an earlier letter. Although this is a matter of scholarly conjecture, the arguments for a later dating are persuasive.

The dominant images of women are submissive wife and mother. Women are commanded to be subject to their husbands in Col. 3:18 and Eph. 5:22. Obedience to the husband as God's chosen authority is a message to be passed on from older women to younger ones in Titus 2:5. The relationship between the head and the body is used as an analogy both for the relationship of Christ to the church and the husband to the wife. This analogy has had lasting implications for women in the Christian tradition. Men were identified with the spirit and mind while women were associated with that which was sensual, "earthy," and related to physical needs and desires.

These letters also provide a theological rationale for the subordination of female to male that goes beyond that which Paul suggests in 1 Corinthians 11. The First and Second Letters to Timothy attribute this status to the fact that woman was created after man and that she was easily deceived by the devil. Second Timothy 3:6 reflects this by declaring that false beliefs may be spread by weak women throughout the community. First Timothy suggests that women may compensate for this transgression through obedience in marriage and childbearing. The option of celibacy to work for the kingdom of God is not presented.

Appropriate behavior for women in the churches is also prescribed. First Corinthians 14 and 1 Timothy 2 prohibit women from speaking or teaching and from exercising any kind of authority in the congregations. Questions on religious matters were to be discussed at home under the guidance of a wise husband. The bishop is defined carefully as "the husband of one wife" and is to be judged by his success in exercising patriarchal authority over his own household. Thus, the leadership of the Christian churches is defined as male. The restrictions placed on women in these sources eventually came to be the normal pattern for the Christian community.

What were the reasons behind the curtailment of female leadership in the early communities? The early churches throughout the Greco-Roman world inherited the institutional structure of the Jewish synagogue. The synagogues were governed by groups of elected elders who were men, reflecting the patriarchal character of first-century Judaism. Women, as we have seen, had no role in the public affairs of the synagogue and attended worship in segregated seating areas. It is likely that the early churches were overcome by inherited customs and prejudices regarding the status of women.[4]

Also, by the time the letters discussed in this section were composed, the churches had begun to realize that the end of the world was not upon them. Instead, they had to prepare for a long stay in the world and this meant coming to terms with Greco-Roman culture, in which most congregations found themselves. That culture was often hostile to Christianity, charging it with secret cannibalism and disloyalty to the Roman emperor, and imposing harsh penalties upon its supporters. The dominant culture was also experiencing turmoil as the patriarchal patterns of Rome and Greece were being challenged by new legislation which gave women certain social rights. The early Christians may have wished to draw as little attention to themselves as possible in this hostile and insecure environment. They adopted traditional cultural views on appropriate behavior for women and in so doing effectively stifled female leadership in the churches.[5]

THE MINISTRIES OF WOMEN IN THE POST-BIBLICAL CHURCHES

Sacramental and Teaching Ministries

It is not clear whether women functioned as presbyters in the early churches and whether they baptized and celebrated the Lord's Supper. There are fragments of information from archaeological discoveries that suggest a wide role for women in these early years. Some Greek-language tombstones that refer to women as presbyters have been located, although it is not certain whether these women were presbyters in Jewish or Christian congregations. Also, one fresco from a Roman catacomb appears to depict a group of women jointly celebrating the Lord's Supper, probably during a catacomb vigil to mark the anniversary of the death of a Christian friend. The figures are all characterized by upswept hair, slender necks, sloping shoulders, and a hint of earrings. The figure actually breaking the bread is clothed in distinctive female dress.

The vehemence and frequency with which the teaching and sacramental functions of women are denounced also suggest that these activities may have been going on in some places. By the end of the second century, the writings of theologians and pastors as well as books of discipline and church order repeatedly condemn such activities. The need for repetition may bear witness to the continued failure of such commands. Manuals such as the *Didascalia Apostolorum* (a book of church order from Syria written between A.D. 200 and 250) and *Apostolic Church Order* (a document regulating church practices from Egypt, written around A.D. 300) prohibit women from baptizing or conducting the Lord's Supper. The general message was that women could not exercise authority over men and could not speak in the church's public gatherings. Although some leaders permitted women to instruct other women in private and their husbands at home, others forbade women even to write about their faith because this was similar to teaching.

The exclusion of women from teaching and sacramental ministries was caused by a number of factors. The biblical tradition was widely interpreted as supporting female subordination and silence. Especially extensive use was made of concepts such as the creation of woman after man and her responsibility for the first sin as well as the command in 1 Timothy (believed to be from the apostle Paul) that women be quiet and submissive in the churches. The *Apostolic Constitutions* (a body of church law coming from Syria in the fourth century) claims that women were not permitted "to stand" with the apostles at the Last Supper. A number of church orders and theologians make the point that Jesus did not commission any women to teach and baptize and that women could not teach men who were in authority or "at the head" over them.

A less frequently articulated but nevertheless real concern of early churchmen was the fear that menstruating women would somehow pollute the worship and sacraments of the church. Ancient cultures regarded menstruating women with fear and suspicion. We can only speculate on reasons for this. The monthly cycle may have linked women with cosmic forces because it resembled the cycle of the moon. Blood was almost universally regarded as a mysterious, awe-full life force—yet women bled and did not die. Whatever the reasons, menstruation was seen as giving women power and this power was believed to be evil and destructive ultimately. Women were viewed as a source of foul contamination. It was even feared that sexual intercourse with a menstruating woman would cause castration. Women were isolated from the community each month and rigid controls were placed on them.

These attitudes passed into Judaism and eventually into Christianity. A bishop of Alexandria, Dionysius the Great, was the first Christian leader to urge that restrictions be placed on menstruating women. Subsequent church councils repeated his view that "impure persons" should not be allowed near the altar. In some places, this prohibition was extended to say that menstruating women should not even enter a church. During the seventh century, for example, one archbishop of Canterbury proclaimed that "women shall not in the time of impurity enter into a church, or communicate."[6]

Finally, if women ever exercised sacramental and teaching ministries, they were probably eased out as the church underwent certain organizational changes. In the early decades of church history, the "ministry" included a variety of tasks and all the members of the community. The Holy Spirit, who acted through the community but was not bound by it, gave the gifts needed to fulfill these distinctive services. By the fourth century, however, a gradual shift in the church's concept of ministry and in its organizational structure had started to occur. The church became more hierarchical. A superior "ministry," which included teaching and sacramental functions, began to emerge over and above an inferior "laity." The church took as its organizational model the civil service of the Roman Empire. More and more power was vested in the offices of bishop and presbyter or priest, and those who filled them were selected by other members in positions of power. Because of its bias against placing women in positions of authority and superiority, it was impossible for the Christian community to select women as bishops and presbyters.[7]

Female Prophets

There were some ministries, however, in which women were clearly involved and which, in some places, continued long after female teaching and sacramental functions were discouraged. Women, for example, filled the role of prophet in the early churches. The prophets were not formally ordained or appointed by the congregations but were the recipients of immediate revelation and inspiration from the Holy Spirit. They were not attached to a single community but instead wandered from place to place. In some instances, it seems that they presided over the life and worship of individual congregations. The *Didache*, a manual of church order from the second century, claims that the traveling prophets filled a role of great importance and that many celebrated the Lord's Supper. The four daughters of Philip were prophets (Acts 21:9) who ministered first in Caesarea and then moved to Hierapolis in Asia Minor. The female prophet from Thyatira in Rev. 2:20 is portrayed as holding great power in the community.

Female Deacons

Women also served as deacons in the early Christian churches. Male deacons were part of the church structure by the end of the first century. They cared for the needy, prepared new converts for baptism, read the Scriptures in worship, and distributed the Lord's Supper. As assistants to the bishop and under his authority, they were set apart to serve (*diakonein*) the community. Evidence for the existence of female deacons in the earliest congregations, however, is ambiguous. First Timothy 3:11 may refer to both men and women when it gives instructions for the appropriate behavior of deacons. Also, a letter written by Pliny, the governor of Bithynia, claims that he tortured two young Christian women who were called *ministrae* or ministers in their community. If women were deacons in the earliest years of Christian history, their duties are not clear. They may have been identical to those of the male deacons.

By the end of the third century, however, women deacons or "deaconesses" filled a special role in many places in the early Christian world. Both manuscript evidence and archaeological inscriptions coming from the Eastern churches in places such as Jerusalem, Syria, Greece, and Asia Minor give a clear record of the existence and nature of this ministry. At first the women were appointed by the bishop from the entire congregation, although as time passed they were required to be virgins or widows. Their main tasks were aimed at keeping the church from harmful scandal in a hostile culture. The women deacons visited sick women in their homes and anointed women at the time of their baptism. They also received baptized women when they emerged from the water. In all of these situations, the church feared that male deacons might be exposed to nude or semi-clothed females. Some early Christian literature gave additional duties to the women deacons. They were to distribute charity to poor women, find seats for women in the church, and act as intermediaries between women and the male clergy. Sometimes they were even charged with the responsibility of teaching recently baptized women about the Christian life.

In many places between the third and sixth centuries, women deacons were regarded as part of the "clergy," and they were ordained to their office. The procedure for this ritual in the church orders follows that for the male deacons. The *Apostolic Constitutions*, for example, contains the following prayer for the ordination of a woman to the office of deacon: "O Eternal God, . . . the Creator of man and of woman, who replenished with the Spirit Miriam, and Deborah, and Anna and Huldah . . . do Thou now also look down upon this Thy servant who is to be ordained to the office of a deaconess, and grant her Thy Holy Spirit. . . . "[8] Despite the fact that these women were ordained to a clerical office, they were excluded from some of the tasks the male deacons performed. They did not assist, for example, at the Lord's Supper. In some of the church orders, they were specifically forbidden to carry out activities reserved for the bishops, presbyters, and male deacons. At the baptismal ceremony, they were barred from pronouncing the baptismal formula.

Widows

Another role for women which is dealt with extensively in early Christian literature is that of widow. Originally widows were simply the worthy recipients of charity from the churches. They had to be known for their righteous lives and completely without other resources. They were enrolled or registered throughout the early centuries of church history as eligible for donations along with orphans and strangers.

In the third century, however, widows also begin to appear in many places as members of a special "order" to which they were "appointed." To qualify for this special appointment, a woman generally had to be over sixty (fifty in some places) and married only once. She was obligated to live a life of complete chastity. She was not ordained but simply "appointed" or "named," often in a simple public ritual. Her main task was that of prayer for the whole church and for her benefactors. Behind this task was the ancient belief that God heard the prayers of the widowed and oppressed. The widow was thought to be particularly effective in praying for the sick and she was sometimes encouraged to lay hands on the sick. Frequent fasting became an additional obligation accompanying prayer in some places. The widow exercised no liturgical ministry, although in some literature her function involved the teaching of younger women who were new to the Christian faith.

The *Testamentum Domini Nostri Jesu Christi* (a Syrian work from the second half of the fifth century) gives the appointed widows an unusually exalted position in the churches. It claims that "a widow is ordained after having been chosen."⁹ The theologian Tertullian argued that widows were entitled to occupy special seating in the church as "ecclesiastical dignitaries." The *Testamentum*, however, goes beyond this by claiming that the widows rightfully deserved a place next to the presbyters who were next to the bishop. During the celebration of the Lord's Supper, they were to move behind the veil hiding the sacrament along with the other clergy. These widows may represent female counterparts to the male presbyters. Both groups carried responsibilities for the well-being of the community, the widows through prayer and the presbyters through wise governance.

WOMEN OUTSIDE THE ORTHODOX MAINSTREAM

Gnosticism

The status of women in groups that deviated from what became mainstream, orthodox Christianity is also important to us because of the wide opportunities for participation that women seemed to be given. Two of these movements, Gnosticism and Montanism, are especially significant. Gnosticism drew upon a multitude of religious and philosophical ideas circulating at the end of the first century. It was not as much a religious movement as a cluster of movements that had certain beliefs in common. The Gnostics generally believed that a supreme God, who could not be known, differed from the spirit that created the material world. Creation was the result of either malice or disobedience toward the supreme God, and the material world that resulted was evil. In the hubbub of creation, however, sparks of divinity from the supreme God were imprisoned in certain human beings. A redeemer had been sent to release these imprisoned sparks by giving people special knowledge (gnosis) of the existence of the supreme God and the true origins of the world.

Gnosticism had a profound impact upon the interpretation given to the life and work of Jesus in many places. The gnostic Christians argued that Jesus was the redeemer who had been sent to pass on this special knowledge necessary for salvation to his apostles. They backed up their ideas by appealing to certain parts of the New Testament as well as to special books which they believed to contain material handed down by the apostles.

The exact role played by women in the gnostic groups is uncertain. There are indications in some texts that women may have been prominent in the communities and regarded in an authoritative light. In the *Gospel of Mary*, for example, Mary Magdalene is given a special revelation by Jesus and is urged to teach it to the other disciples. In a later gnostic book, *Pistis Sophia*, Mary is also given an important role. Jesus' words in this text are, "But Mary Magdalene and John, the maiden, will surpass all my disciples . . . , they will be on my right hand and on my left and I am they and they are I. . . . "[10] In both of these gnostic texts, the patriarchal trend of the early church, which would become dominant, is represented in the words of Peter, who rebukes Mary for her brashness and doubts the legitimacy of her message. There is also evidence that women were permitted to function as prophets, teachers, priests, and even bishops in some gnostic circles. This practical equality may have been based on gnostic descriptions of God as containing masculine and feminine dimensions.

Montanism

Montanus and two women, Priscilla and Maxima, led another religious movement which developed at the end of the second century. The Montanists, as their followers came to be called, enthusiastically proclaimed the Christian message, believing themselves to be channels for divine truth. They preached that the end of the world was near and they encouraged Christians to seek persecution actively. There is evidence in the Montanist movement that women were given access to leadership positions and were able to perform many of the tasks reserved for the bishop and presbyter. Women such as Priscilla were held in great honor as "prophetesses." The Montanists believed that since Eve was the first to eat of the tree of knowledge, women were more likely than men to be recipients of divine wisdom and revelation. Above all, however, the Montanists did not discriminate on the basis of sex because of Paul's statement that "in Christ, there is neither male nor female."

Orthodox Responses

A strong school of thought in the early church opposed both gnostic Christianity and Montanism. This opposing tradition came to be regarded as the "orthodox" or "catholic" tradition while the other groups were denounced as "heretical." In the case of Gnosticism, orthodox Christians were certainly offended by the ideas that the created world was evil and that Jesus was not truly human. In the case of Montanism, the movement's encouragement of martyrdom was seen as suicidal to the growth of the church. Yet we must at least consider the possibility that orthodox Christianity, which had already succumbed to its male-dominated cultural environment, excluded and persecuted the Gnostics and Montanists because of the varied roles they gave to women. At the same time, mainline Catholic Christianity became more concerned to keep women silent and subordinate so as to avoid any identification with the heretical groups. Consequently, a struggle against Gnosticism may be reflected in the letters to Timothy and Titus and a struggle against Montanism may be behind the disappearance of the women prophets in Christian history.

MARTYRDOM AND THE WITNESS OF PERPETUA

The early Christian communities were subjected to periods of persecution during the first centuries of their existence. Women shared in these sufferings along with men. Their participation is clearly described in the few available statistical records of persecution and in literature on the lives of the martyrs. From these sources we learn that the experience of martyrdom was essentially the same for men and women. Women gave in to their torturers, and women willingly died. Women emerged as leaders among those who were put to death because of their beliefs. Only in the content of their prophetic visions of their future battles and victories do the women differ from the men. Their visions are more likely to contain descriptions of flowers and gardens as well as concern for modesty, personal appearance, and other people.

One such period of persecution occurred in Carthage from 202–203. Those Christians who refused to worship the gods of the Roman Empire were singled out for punishment. Saturus, a Christian teacher, and five of his newly-baptized pupils were arrested. Among them was Perpetua, the daughter of a wealthy civil servant, and her slave girl, Felicitas. Perpetua left a remarkable written record of the experience of martyrdom in the early church.[11] Her work was later given an introduction and conclusion by an editor and circulated for many years among congregations. It represents the earliest known piece of Christian literature written by a woman. It allows us to glimpse not only her understanding of Christianity but also her view of the society in which she lived and her role among the other Christian prisoners.

Perpetua's document is dominated by the themes of protest and liberation.[12] Her protest is against a society that handed out injustice and oppression to human beings. The treatment of women as deferential wives and daughters and as machines to replenish the population was a part of this total picture. Perpetua believed that she was liberated from the law of the Romans and the expectations of her culture by God who was the highest authority. Her loyalty to Jesus Christ enabled her to transcend her identity as a female or a citizen of a particular nation. This new identity is reflected in her family relationships, her life in prison among the other Christians, and in the images that both she and the editor use to describe her character.

Perpetua rejects the domestic norms to which she is expected to conform in two important ways. She disregards the pleas of her aged father who constantly visits her in prison and urges her to compromise her beliefs. She also gives up her newborn son, whom she has been nursing in prison, to her father, thus relinquishing her responsibilities as mother rather than give in to the Roman authorities. In both of these instances, her family ties are not broken lightly but with great sadness and suffering. She describes her appearance before the governor, Hilarion, in the following words: "Hilarion . . . said, 'Have pity on your father's grey head; have pity on your infant son; offer sacrifice for the emperors' welfare.' But I answered, 'I will not.' Hilarion asked, 'Are you a Christian?' And I answered, 'I am a Christian.' And when my father persisted in his attempts to dissuade me, Hilarion ordered him thrown out and he was beaten with a rod. My father's injury hurt me as much as if I myself had been beaten."[13]

Among the Christians in prison, Perpetua also emerges as a figure of authority who has been claimed by the Holy Spirit. "My brother said to me, 'Dear sister, you already have such a great reputation in that you could ask for a vision indicating whether you will be condemned or freed.' Since I knew that I could speak with the Lord, whose great favors I had already experienced, I confidently promised to do so."[14] She experiences a series of prophetic visions which assure her friends that a new and far better life awaited them after death and that they would be victorious over their fears and their persecutors. In her visions as well as in those of Saturus, Perpetua is also raised to a position of spiritual authority over the male clergy who were beginning to emerge as a powerful force in the church. Her salvation comes to her through her fight with the powers of evil, aided only by Christ and not by the official ministers.

During her days in prison, Perpetua also transcends her identity as a dependent wife and mother by assuming both masculine and feminine characteristics. She is called "the true spouse of Christ" and the "darling of God" on the day of her martyrdom. She is described as sister, mother, and daughter and she acts with gentleness, tenderness, and maternal compassion. But she is also a leader and warrior who is strong, fierce, and bold. She chides the jailers for their inhumanity, slyly arguing that it would reflect well on them if the martyrs stayed in good physical condition since they would appear in the arena on Caesar's birthday. In one of her visions of her coming battle with the forces of evil, she sees herself as a man who is stripped of his clothing and rubbed with oil for combat. In this same vision she sees herself as the peaceful daughter who is given the branch of victory. Perpetua represents the Christian who is freed from society's expectations of women and men.

The account of Perpetua was circulated widely in the early churches for purposes of instruction and inspiration. Parts of her story were read as part of the official liturgy in many places. The anniversary of her death became the occasion for special celebrations, a basilica was dedicated to her in Carthage, and Augustine, the Bishop of Hippo, preached several sermons in her honor. Gradually, however, the memory of Perpetua faded in the Christian tradition. This was partly due to the prominence of earlier martyrs who were leading bishops but it may also have been caused by the growing power of the male clergy who considered the writings of a woman inadequate and improper for official church use.

Patristic Attitudes Toward Women

Attitudes toward women in the Christian tradition even in the twentieth century have been shaped in no small way by a number of theological writers who lived in the first six centuries of Christian history. The influence wielded by these men is reflected in their designation as the "fathers of the church." They had a variety of vocations and lived in many geographic locations throughout the Greco-Roman world. Clement of Alexandria, for example, was a teacher. Jerome was a biblical scholar and secretary to Pope Damasus I. Augustine was bishop of the North African city of Hippo. The church fathers included other prominent figures in the church hierarchy as well as in the monastic communities.

The life, death, and resurrection of Jesus was central to their work, but they had to convey and explain the message of the gospel in terms that would be compatible with the thought patterns of the Greco-Roman world. There was a strong tendency in this culture to divide reality into two opposing or contradictory spheres, the sphere of mind and spirit and the sphere of the body or flesh. The mind and spirit was identified with that which was good or virtuous while the flesh was represented as that which had to be overcome or conquered. Sometimes this line of thought condemned the body and the material world as hopelessly evil and corrupt. It deeply influenced the growth of the ascetic spirit within the churches (see chap. 3).

This "dualistic" approach to the world, as it was called, had an influence on the way in which women were regarded. They were identified traditionally with the body while the mind was seen as essentially masculine. The result was an association of the female with the flesh, the material world, and the drive to satisfy physical desires and, therefore, with that which was evil.

The church fathers certainly make statements that degrade women and the feminine. Such ideas have been picked up and quoted at length by people in the Christian community who have tried to keep women silent and subordinate. Yet these Christian theologians could not ignore the Christian doctrine of the goodness of creation, the blessing of God on married life, and the equality between male and female which Paul proclaims. Their works relevant to women therefore are not only numerous but also complex. We can, however, suggest some of the major ideas that emerge on the nature of women, virginity, and the married life.

Women Prone to Sin

One prominent belief in the church fathers is that women are responsible for sin in the world. Many turn to the Genesis story to substantiate this, although some of the writers such as Tertullian and Ambrose sometimes describe the first sin as a joint responsibility. The fathers also see women as a continuing source of sin in the world since they seduce men away from the "heights" of mind and spirit to a lower concern for physical satisfaction and pleasure.

As a potential source of sin and danger to the spiritual well-being of the community, women are to be kept subordinate in church and society. While some of these theologians regarded subordination as the penalty for Eve's sin, Augustine taught that woman was created as inferior to man. He argued that woman was created with a mind and spirit that were weak and readily overcome by strong physical passion. Even in the garden therefore the male was to rule, govern, and teach.

The church fathers also make it clear that men and women are equally redeemed by baptism in Christ. In terms of their souls before God, gender was irrelevant. Even for Christian women, however, spiritual equality could have no counterpart in the concrete life of family, church, and nation. Although Christian women might have interior purity, they were still bound to the flesh which could seduce and succumb to physical pleasure.

Both Christian men and women are advised to adopt a life style of chastity and modesty in a number of these treatises. The instructions for women are particularly lengthy and explicit. The behavior of the Christian woman was meant to contrast sharply with the behavior of women in the urban centers of the decaying Roman Empire. The Christian woman is to stop using makeup (the work of the devil) and she is to avoid wearing jewelry. She is to wear a veil to signify her subjection and she is not to appear in silk dresses which would show the shape of her body. She is to seclude herself at home and be careful not to visit the public baths.

Marriage and Sexuality

None of the church fathers condemns married life as evil and against the will of God, although Jerome comes close to doing this in a strong plea for the virgin life. Married life is treated generally with delicacy and sensitivity. Some of the fathers stress that husband and wife should live in a relationship of love and trust. They encourage the marriage partners to serve each other and to fulfill their mutual responsibilities. They contrast the Christian marriage to that of the non-Christian in which passion rules the domineering husband and the lusty wife.

There is a strong tendency in these works, however, to see sexual union as tainted with sin. Some of the fathers claim that God's original creation consisted of a single spiritual being who had no sexual characteristics, while others believe that male and female characteristics were part of the perfect creation but were not to result in sexual union. This union became a reality only after sin entered the world. Augustine argued that sexual union did take place in paradise but without lust and under the complete control of the male will and mind. After the Fall, however, lust took over and not only passed on original sin to the offspring but tarnished the relationship between man and woman as well.

The Virgin Life

Augustine and the earlier writer Clement of Alexandria both approved of sexual intercourse to produce children. The union, however, should be the product of the will and not the passions. More commonly, Christians were urged to avoid marriage and sexual intercourse entirely. The life of virginity was celebrated as infinitely preferable to all other marital states. The virgin was regarded as possessing the most important "charism" or gift from the Holy Spirit. Mothers were urged to dedicate their daughters to the chaste life. Jerome even taught that the only possible justification for sexual union was the production of more virgins: from coitus came virgins just as from thorns came roses and from shells came pearls.

Some of the church fathers suggest practical reasons for choosing the virgin life. Tertullian claims that it freed men and women to be martyrs. Other writers argue that the monastic life offered women protection in a brutal society. Jerome, in his effort to advocate chastity, gives lurid descriptions of married life to deter young men and women. He asks men why they would want to get involved with the perpetual whining and nagging of a wife, and he describes to women the discomforts of pregnancy and the pain of childbirth.

Aside from these practical reasons, many of the church fathers provide theological support for their celebration of the virgin life. Both men and women who chose this life anticipated or had a "head start" on the life that awaited them in the kingdom of God. Christians in the kingdom would be given spiritual bodies like those of the angels, without sexual characteristics. For some of the writers, the virgins were also concrete examples of God's original creation which would be restored in the future kingdom. By erasing their sexuality, male or female, they already participated to some extent in a new order of reality.

In the church fathers, virginity became the one channel in the Christian community through which women could acquire some measure of practical equality with men. The price a woman paid was dear: she was to obliterate her "femaleness" (see chap. 3). She did this by denying her childbearing ability, by fasting to eliminate her menstrual period, and by making herself as unattractive as possible. The equality baptism brought to women in the earliest decades of the church's history was restored in part in the virgin life. The church fathers along with many other men speak highly of the learning and dedication of these women. Jerome, for example, praises the biblical scholarship of the virgin circle in Rome as well as their rigor in denying themselves physical pleasures. Women in this life could be allowed some measure of authority and freedom because they no longer represented the powerful "lower nature" which could lure men away from the virtuous life of mind and spirit.

WRITERS, POETS, AND PILGRIMS

The account of Perpetua's martyrdom is only one of several religious works written by women in the early years of Christian history. While later female writers generally come from religious orders or monastic communities, some of these early women are married and all are from the upper classes of Roman society. The content and style of their works are varied, but all made some contribution to knowledge of the Christian faith. Examples of this can be seen in Proba's *Cento* and Egeria's manuscript describing her trip to the Holy Land.[15]

Proba's Cento

Proba was a matron of the prominent and wealthy Anicii family. She probably became a convert to Christianity sometime in her adult life. Like other women of the Roman privileged classes, she had a great deal of leisure time and she used some of it for the study of classical culture and for writing. Her *Cento* was probably written sometime around A.D. 351.

Cento was a popular form of poetry in the Greco-Roman world. The author of a cento borrowed lines and half-lines from the works of a master poet such as Virgil or Homer and arranged them to suit his or her own purposes. Although this appears like plagiarism to us, it was considered to be a high form of praise for the master poet. Proba rearranged parts of Virgil's works on secular subjects in order to tell the biblical story. The first part describes the history of Israel up to the giving of the Law. Then Proba jumps to the life of Jesus, using the verse of Virgil to describe events such as the slaughter of the firstborn in Egypt, the storm on the lake, and the last supper.

Although the *Cento* does remain faithful to orthodox views on Jesus, Proba omits large portions of the gospel story and misinterprets others in her effort to patch Virgil together. Her work was not given a favorable reception by church authorities in Rome but it continued for centuries to be used as a textbook for the instruction of boys.

Proba's *Cento* is also significant because it represents a challenge to the exclusion of women from the creation of a Christian theological tradition. In her own way, Proba was attempting to do what the church fathers were doing: interpret Jesus to the Greco-Roman world in familiar thought patterns. Many Roman citizens found the language of the Bible clumsy and they were still suspicious and hostile toward Christianity. Proba's *Cento* tried to bridge this gap.

Egeria's Pilgrimage to the Holy Land

A literary work of an entirely different kind from the pen of a woman was discovered at the end of the nineteenth century in the library of an Italian monastery. The manuscript describes a pilgrimage made to the Holy Land, probably in the early fifth century. Scholars believe that the account was written by Egeria.

The only information we have about Egeria must be inferred from her manuscript itself. In it there is evidence that she was a wealthy woman: she was on the pilgrimage for several years, she traveled with an extensive entourage, and she was given preferential treatment in many places by those in authority. Egeria reveals herself as well-read in the Scriptures. She frequently discussed the Bible with her hosts and she tried to interpret her travels in light of the biblical story. She bombards the Bishop of Carrae, who was "very learned in Scripture," with a whole series of questions about the geographic movements of Abraham's family including "where the well was from which Saint Jacob gave water to the sheep which were herded by Rachel the daughter of Laban the Syrian."[16] It is probable that Egeria belonged to a group of virgin women who were bound together by strong ties of affection, who studied the Bible together, and who had some responsibility for seeing that the worship in their church was conducted properly. She frequently refers to her readers as "ladies," "my venerable sisters," and "my light." They were not members of a religious or monastic order and there is no hint in Egeria's account that she lived a life of poverty.

The account itself is really a travel diary describing a pilgrimage which lasted a long period of time. The first half of the manuscript relates her journey from Mt. Sinai to Constantinople (along with many side trips) while the second part gives a detailed account of the forms of worship used in the Jerusalem church. Egeria's work is not simply a catalogue of places but provides insights into local practices, people, and traditions which are often missing in travel diaries. Her work is of great value because of the information it provides on early Christian worship and architecture and on the condition of the biblical sites in the fifth century.

During her pilgrimage Egeria stops at the shrine of St. Thecla near Selucium. Thecla was celebrated in the early church as a missionary who had been converted by Paul and commissioned by him to teach. In the *Acts of Paul and Thecla* (in circulation by the end of the second century) she breaks off her engagement and, in the face of violent family opposition, adopts the virgin life. As female leadership was curtailed in the early churches and the roles of widow, deacon, and prophetess disappeared, the virgin life became an important source of female power and male approval. In medieval Christianity, the "good woman" was a virgin while all other women were associated by nature with the powers of darkness.

CHAPTER 3

VIRGIN AND WITCH: WOMEN IN MEDIEVAL CHRISTIANITY

The images of women that emerge in medieval literature were shaped to a large extent by monks, bishops, and noblemen who comprised that small percentage of the population that was literate. Images of women in both secular and church writings oscillate between two extreme positions which historians have described as "the pit and the throne." On the one hand, women are denounced in strong terms as wicked and inferior. This virulent misogynism (a hatred and distrust of women) reached its peak in the witch craze which swept across Europe from the fifteenth to the eighteenth centuries. On the other hand, women are praised, idealized, and adored in the symbol of the Virgin Mary and as the courtly lady in the popular tales of chivalry.

Many medieval theologians repeat some of the main ideas on women found in the church fathers. Thomas Aquinas, for example, claimed that woman was created as subordinate and inferior to man. Not only was she second in the order of creation, but she was endowed with less intellectual capability and, consequently, less ability to make right moral decisions. Aquinas and others also propagated the belief that women were more sensual than men and more oriented toward the functions and appetites of the human body. Based on the revival of certain Greek ideas, Aquinas added that women were "defective" human beings. They were the result of an accident to the male sperm which would always produce another male under normal circumstances.

A fear of women and their power to cause lust and sin in men permeated not only theology but popular piety as well. Stories about adulterous wives far outnumbered those of unfaithful husbands. Books of "wikked wives" detailed all the women in the Bible and in history who had led men astray. The widespread vices of women were constantly stressed as well as the need to keep women under control in church and society. The monastic literature frequently portrayed women as talking too much, causing discord, loving gold, and being disloyal. Literature addressed to young women urged them to honor and obey their husbands, even when their husbands were evil. Church law specifically permitted wife beating as a way to control female corruption and disobedience.

A few positive attitudes toward women did find their way into medieval theology. Aquinas and others stressed that women, although inferior, had been given the important task of procreation by God. Some theologians also insisted that men and women have rational souls and that in the future kingdom of God, male and female would be "equivalent." The institution of marriage itself was also given a slightly more positive character. Marriage was increasingly described as a "sacrament" which conferred God's grace upon those bound in it. Virginity, however, was still applauded as the best life style for women since it dissociated them from sexuality and therefore from evil.

THE LIFE OF VIRGINITY AND CHASTITY

The Growth of Asceticism

By the end of the third century, a growing number of Christians were adopting a life style of asceticism. They denied themselves physical pleasures such as eating and warmth, doing only what was necessary to stay alive. They practiced voluntary poverty and complete abstinence from sexual relations. This "practice" or "exercise" of self-discipline (from which the word "asceticism" comes) was seen as both a good preparation for martyrdom and a way to a more holy or perfect life in the eyes of God. Less time and resources spent in the preparation of food and on personal appearance meant more time and resources for prayer, worship, and acts of charity. Some Christians also believed that the kingdom of God and the end of time would be brought nearer if the followers of Jesus practiced self-denial.

Christian ascetics looked to the biblical tradition to justify their life style. The Old Testament does recommend periods of fasting and sexual abstinence, but overall it applauds the goodness of the created world and married life. In the examples and teachings of Jesus and Paul, however, the ascetics believed that they found strong support. Jesus told his disciples that they must deny themselves and follow him. His life was one of a poor nomad who had no possessions and who lived a life of complete chastity. Paul frequently spoke of the need to quell the passions of the flesh. He endured nakedness and cold for the gospel and, above all, he counseled that celibacy is preferable to marriage. Christian asceticism gained further impetus from prevalent philosophies in Greco-Roman culture. Some of these philosophies not only advised the avoidance of physical pleasure, but they also expressed a contempt for the material world as evil which went far beyond biblical teachings.

Monastic and Domestic Asceticism

Many women as well as men adopted the ascetic way of life in the Christian community. Some were widows who vowed to live in perfect chastity and self-denial for the remainder of their lives. Others were married women who persuaded their husbands to relinquish sexual relations and live together in chastity. Still others were young unmarried women who eventually were referred to as "virgins." The virgins are occasionally mentioned in writings from the second century but it was not until the following century that they were recognized as a special order within the community. They were not ordained to their role since virginity was not seen as an office bestowed by the church but rather one that was privately and voluntarily chosen. The women made a private vow to live the virgin life, although this vow was complemented by a public ritual in later church history.

The virgins were regarded as special symbols for the union of Christ with the church. They were called the "brides" or "spouses" of Christ because they had entered into a mystical union with him. A virgin who broke her vow was considered to be guilty of adultery in both church law and civil law. In some places, she was punished by death. An illustration of this understanding of virginity comes from the life of Macrina, a leader of one of the earliest communities of women ascetics. She lived a chaste life with no possessions and was buried in a beautiful wedding gown at the time of her death.

Christianity was established as the state religion of the Roman Empire in the fourth century. The churches filled with members who had only a passing or halfhearted interest in Christianity. The ascetic life became an attractive option for those who wished to escape from lax standards of faith and practice. Women again opted for the ascetic life which was taking several distinctive forms. Women became hermits, virgins in their own homes, partners in "spiritual marriages," and members of monastic communities.

Domestic Asceticism. Many women chose to live the life of chastity in their own homes. This was a particularly attractive option for wealthy women who could remain in seclusion on their estates or gather around them female friends, relatives, and servants of a similar spirit. Early Christian pastors and theologians were concerned with the problems the "virgins of the world" faced. They dispensed advice on the kind of company these women should keep, the clothes they should wear in order to avoid attention, and the strategy they should use in dealing with family pressure to marry. Women with property faced subtle and sometimes violent attempts to persuade them to abandon their vows and prevent family wealth from passing into the hands of the church.

The Monastic Community. The ancient historian Palladius records that there were some twenty thousand women living in poverty, chastity, and solitude in the desert surrounding Egypt. Whatever the actual numbers, the life of the desert hermit was less frequently chosen than the organized community life of the monastery. From the fourth century on, monasteries for women proliferated throughout the Christian world. Some shared a roof with a male community, others were separate but close to male monasteries, and some existed on their own. The monastery became a popular option for virgin women as Christian history unfolded. In it, women lived under the authority of a superior or leader and according to certain regulations of life style set out in the monastic "rule." One such rule was developed for men and women who lived in two monastic communities in Egypt. It illustrates the daily life and responsibilities of some four hundred women in this particular group. The women spent most of their time in a routine of worship, prayer, and Scripture study. These contemplative tasks which had been done by the widows in the churches were gradually taken over in the monastic communities. Also, the women made their own clothing and clothing for their male counterparts across the river. Many other female communities shared this basic division of the day into periods for household tasks and periods for devotion.

The Spiritual Marriage. Another life style chosen by women was the "spiritual marriage" in which a man and a woman committed to a life of chastity shared the same house and sometimes the same bed. The couple engaged in an intimate but not sexual relationship. There are many condemnations of this practice in the writings of early bishops and theologians and many church councils forbid it right through the Middle Ages. The assumption of course was that men and women could not cohabit and at the same time be faithful to their vows of chastity. Yet these "spiritual marriages" met a need for women who did not live near a monastery and who were not wealthy in their own right. They could, in this arrangement, depend on a man of similar ideals to provide a livelihood and some protection. Also, the *agapatae* (as Jerome called these women) seemed to share a deep friendship with their male partners which Greco-Roman culture believed to be impossible between men and women. They raise for the Christian community the possibility of relationships between men and women that are other than sexual and yet still intimate and compassionate.

Power and Authority in the Virgin Life

The ascetic life offered women certain opportunities for choice, freedom, and participation from which they were excluded in church and society. In practical terms, communal life gave women physical protection both from the risks of childbearing and from the risks of living alone in a society that looked on unmarriageable and dangerous women the rule of Rome is integrated.

Throughout Christian history, the ascetic life also often gave women eling on their name of religion. Melania the Younger, for example, traveled throughout Africa and Palestine. The Holy Land was a favorite destination. Wherever these ascetic women traveled, they were greeted

The monasteries for women were also headed by women, giving them an opportunity to exercise authority and leadership within the institutional sphere of the Christian community. The list of women in this capacity begins with individuals such as Paula, the associate of Jerome, and the sister of Augustine, and extends throughout Christian history. The medieval abbesses, however, most clearly illustrate the temporal (relating to the affairs of this world) as well as spiritual power that the monastic life offered to women.

The abbess usually headed a group of women living the monastic life under some form of the rule designed by Saint Benedict in the sixth century. In countries such as England and northern France, they frequently headed "double" monasteries of men and women. In many places, they enjoyed the same powers and privileges as abbots, bishops, and noblemen. They sat in parliaments, attended church councils, and signed official church decrees. They oversaw the affairs of the clergy and lay people who lived on the often vast lands owned by the abbey, and they answered only to the Pope in Rome, not to the local bishop who had no jurisdiction over their territory (this is the origin of the term "exempt order"). The word "ordination" is sometimes used to describe the consecration of an abbess. Although she was not given the power to administer the sacraments, she was given the same signs of high office that a bishop received. These included a ring, mitre (a special headdress worn by bishops and abbots), and crozier (a staff resembling a shepherd's crook carried by bishops and abbots as a symbol of office). In addition to offering spiritual guidance, the abbesses heard the confessions of those in their charge and, despite the wrath of the church hierarchy, even administered penance and granted absolution for sins.

The power of the abbess declined, however, in the later Middle Ages. Double monasteries were closed, their "ordination" became a blessing, and they gradually came under the authority of local bishops. This decline can be attributed in part to a resurgence of patriarchalism in Renaissance culture, with its admiration for ancient Greece and Rome, and in the writings of the Protestant Reformers. This tendency reached its zenith, for the abbesses, in the 1563 decree of the Council of Trent. The exempt female orders were either to join a male order with a male superior or come under the jurisdiction of the local bishop as a delegate of the Pope. Some exempt orders did continue in France, but they were abolished during the aftermath of the French Revolution.[1]

Power Through Piety and Learning. Ascetic women also held positions of authority in a less formal and institutional manner. By virtue of their holiness and personal piety, women were treated frequently with respect and deference by the whole community, including men of high standing among the clergy. Eleanor McLaughlin has described these women as being "empowered" by their holiness.[2] This power was often believed to take concrete form in the ability to perform miracles. Lioba, an eighth-century English ascetic, is recorded as having calmed a storm and healed the sick in her community. She was honored by bishops, nobles, princes, and even the emperor Charlemagne.

Power stemming from a holy life also took shape in the ability to acquire great learning which also attracted men of authority within the church. The ascetic life gave women the opportunity to study and it rewarded them for intellectual achievement. Melania the Younger acquired a formidable theological education, debated doctrine, and taught an array of men and women including the emperor Theodosius. Marcella became an expert on the Bible in Rome and aided the clergy with their dilemmas of translation and interpretation. Lioba was skilled in classical philosophy, theology, and canon law. This erudition, claims one historian, gave her an almost magical authority and prompted the bishop Boniface to seek her help in bringing order to the missionary churches in Germany.

A Chance to Choose. Finally, and perhaps most significantly, the ascetic life gave women an opportunity to exercise free choice and a basis for rejecting the demand that they marry and bear children for the sake of the patriarchal clan. The decision to lead a chaste life was an autonomous one in a society that left little up to the preference of women. Although not all families objected to such a decision, many women experienced family pressures to conform to tradition and many women protested by appealing to the authority of God. In medieval France, for example, Saint Burgundofara hid in a basilica when h^r father wanted to betroth her. When Saint Maxellinda insisted on keeping her vow of chastity even after her marriage, her husband tried to rape and abduct her and eventually murdered her. The experiences of Christina of Markyate provide one of the fullest accounts of a woman's protest and initiative.

Christina, the daughter of an English nobleman, was born at the end of the eleventh century. An account of her life describes her marriage to Burthred despite the fact that she had made a vow to be a virgin when she was thirteen. She refused, however, to consummate the marriage, which was forced on her by her parents. She escaped several plots by her husband and family to lure her into the marriage bed. Once, when her bedroom was invaded by Burthred and his drunken friends, she avoided them by hanging by her fingertips between the bed curtains and the wall. Although Christina initially had the support of the bishop, even he began to pressure her into relenting after receiving a bribe from Christina's father. She eventually escaped from her home disguised as a boy and took up the life of a hermit. Within the medieval Christian community, she became recognized as a woman of power and authority that extended far beyond the confines of her cell.

Medieval Restrictions. The eleventh and twelfth centuries brought a new enthusiasm for Christianity to medieval Europe. One aspect of this revival was a movement to reform the old established monastic orders and to create new orders which emphasized poverty and public preaching reminiscent of the life style of Jesus and his disciples. During this period, a large number of women were attracted to the monastic life. They met with a variety of responses, generally negative, when they tried to open female monasteries under the authority of the reformed and new orders. This negative response was caused largely by the church's views on the nature and role of women.

Some of the new orders initially welcomed women but very quickly abandoned their enthusiasm. The Cistercians (an order established in France in the eleventh century which revived a strict obedience to the monastic rule of St. Benedict) believed that the female sex was not capable of obeying the austere rules and attaining the level of perfection demanded by the order. The Dominicans and Franciscans both had a tradition of encouraging the spirituality of women but soon began to repel any attempts by women to open convents 'under their rules and ministered to by their members. Economic reasons were sometimes given: the men would have to support these new groups of women financially since they frequently came from the lower classes of society and were without wealthy patrons. The argument that close association with women was dangerous to the spiritual well-being of the monks, however, was more evident. As one official document from a new religious order (the Premonstratensians) claimed, "The poisons of vipers and dragons are healthier and less harmful for men than familiarity with women. . . . "³

Some of the new orders that emphasized the public preaching of the gospel, such as that at Fontevrault in France, did welcome women as members but opened convents for them which prevented them from having any contact with the outside world. Obviously, this strategy excluded women from evangelical preaching, which was one of the main activities of the order. There was a growing insistence in the medieval church that women leading the virgin life be locked securely away behind cloistered walls. This opinion was based on the belief that women would easily give in to sexual temptation and would compromise those men with whom they came into contact. Cloistering had long been recommended in some places but in 1299 Pope Boniface VIII tried to impose it upon the whole church. Strict rules were laid down regarding the conversations a monastic woman could have with outsiders as well as the occasions on which she could leave the convent. The Catholic Church tried to enforce this general policy well into the twentieth century.

In some instances, those women who wished to pursue a life of poverty and active mission but who had been refused by the new religious orders joined the Beguines. The Beguines were loosely organized groups of women which emerged mainly in urban areas. The women involved did not take formal vows but did adopt a chaste and simple style of living. They ministered to the poor and sick but despite their good works, the church regarded them with suspicion. Their informality placed them outside the disciplinary structures of the institution and their emphasis on righteous living and a personal relationship to Christ associated them with movements that the church was trying to eliminate.

Ambiguous Space. While the life of chastity and austerity presented new opportunities for power and participation, it did not always have an overall positive effect on the status of women. The monastic community, in fact, represents a somewhat "ambiguous" space for women.⁴ It did not, for example, open up the office of priest and bishop to women. It also suffered from the deep-rooted tendency of the churches to value the writings and lives of the male ascetics above the lives and works of the women. Eleanor McLaughlin suggests that there was a profound difference between the experiences of men and women who entered the religious order.[5] While men were expected to deny themselves sexual experiences, they retained their masculine nature which society defined as superior mental and spiritual capacities. Women, however, were expected to erase their female natures which were closely identified with the functions of procreation. They were encouraged to become "like a man" in their anticipation of the kingdom of God by developing rationality, loyalty, and courage. Also, the celebration of the virgin life tended to degrade women who were not prepared to erase their femaleness and who continued to be wives and mothers. Finally, we are left to ponder whether the monastic ideals of self-denial and self-effacement were appropriate for human beings who had few occasions for pride. The monastic life, in reality, may have hindered the self-development and independence of women and instead reinforced the traits of passiveness and dependence.

MEDIEVAL MARIOLOGY

In contrast to the image of woman as evil seductress, the church as well as medieval society also placed woman on a throne or pedestal as a paragon of virtue and piety. The idealized woman, however, was not a sexual creature. In secular tales of courtly love and chivalry, this image comes across forcefully. In these stories, a beautiful, pure woman is adored by a male lover (not her husband) who in turn is inspired to do great acts of heroism for his lady. No sexual encounter is involved, only spiritual love. The woman stood in a superior position and encouraged morality, patience, and humility in her lover. The church of course had its counterpart to the lady of courtly love in the figure of the Virgin Mary. Especially in the twelfth and thirteenth centuries, the mother of Jesus commanded great devotion and adoration and inspired holy living in many Christians.

Evolution of an Image

The New Testament provides very little information on Mary in contrast to the rich body of story and theology which had accumulated around her by the medieval period. The earliest biblical reference, Gal. 4:4, does not mention Mary directly, but only states that Jesus was born of a woman. Acts 1:14 places her in the community of Christians but the Gospel references describe her relationship to Jesus as ambiguous and peculiar. In some passages, the relationship appears to be tinged with hostility (Mark 3:31–35; John 2:1–11). Only in John's Gospel (19:25–27) does Mary play a role in the last events of Jesus' life.

Luke and Matthew both include Mary in their accounts of the birth of Jesus, but only Luke makes her the center of the drama. Both accounts reveal Mary as an ordinary Palestinian woman who is obedient to the will of God. Both accounts also identify Mary as a virgin at the time of Jesus' birth and they imply that his conception was miraculous. Scholars disagree about the source of this idea which was well established in Christian circles by the time the Gospels were written. It may have come from the Greek version of the Book of Isaiah which prophesied that "a virgin will conceive and bear a son." It may have been borrowed from Greco-Roman culture which ascribed virgin births to its great heroes and leaders to illustrate their divine origins. In any case, for the early church, the virgin birth was probably used to show that Jesus was chosen by God and that he shared both a divine and human nature. It was more a statement about Jesus than about Mary. There is no conclusive biblical evidence that Mary remained a virgin for the duration of her life. That question would be posed by a later age.

In the second century, a cluster of theological ideas and stories about Mary began to grow. Mary's nature and role became the object of intellectual speculation and Mary herself became the focal point of popular devotion.[6] This "cult" of the Virgin Mary was fully developed by the twelfth century. Mary was the Christian counterpart of the romantic lady in medieval tales of chivalry. The cult of Mary was influenced by a number of things: biblical imagery that portrayed Israel as the bride of God and the church as the bride of Christ, pre-Christian goddess worship, and the theological debates over the nature of Jesus.

The virginity of Mary quickly emerged as an essential feature of theology and popular piety. This was especially true as the ascetic lifestyle became more popular. As sexuality became associated with sin, it was necessary to remove sexual relations from the origins of Jesus as the sinless Son of God. Also, those who supported the virgin life used Mary to show that God had placed a seal of approval on chastity.

Virginity was extended from the conception of Jesus to his birth and to Mary's entire life as Christian theology developed. Mary became the perpetual virgin who gave birth to a child without having the seal of her womb, or hymen, broken and who remained a virgin until her death. These ideas were spread by an early Christian book, the *Book of James*, which included many stories about the birth, childhood, and adult life of Mary. Joseph, for example, is portrayed as a widower to explain the existence of the brothers of Jesus in the New Testament.

Apart from virginity, one of the earliest images associated with Mary was that of the New Eve. Mary, it was said, reversed what Eve had done. Eve had broken God's commandments and passed sin and death on to her offspring. Mary, however, was obedient to God and brought redemption to the world through the birth of Jesus. She was the spiritual mother of

Christians who were participants in God's new creation. Mary also represented the whole church or community of believers in her obedience and faith. Both as the New Eve and as the symbol for the church or bride of Christ, Mary took her place in art and literature as the spouse and consort of Jesus who reigned in heaven.

Historians believe that when Christianity became the official religion of the Roman Empire in the fourth century, it was profoundly affected by the beliefs and customs of pre-Christian religions which had been practiced by the new converts. Many of these ancient religions worshiped a mother goddess who was the source of all life and the one from whom the earth, all living creatures, and even the gods themselves derived their being. This goddess devotion may have been transferred to Mary with the coming of Christianity. Particularly, it may be the source of the image of Mary as the Mother of God. This image was reinforced by a strong theological view that said that the divine and human natures of Jesus were intermingled such that it was possible to speak of Mary as the mother of God (God-bearer) and not merely as the mother of the Christ. Mary is still regarded in some agricultural communities as the source of fertility for land and people and the source of good fortune and good weather.

After the first few centuries of Christian history, it became increasingly common to see Jesus as a terrifying judge who was far removed from humanity in his heavenly domain. He was concerned more with punishment for sin rather than with mercy and love. Mary therefore began to assume the role of mediator, speaking on behalf of Christians before God. It was believed that since she had been a human mother, she would not turn away even the most wicked child. She would plead for grace on behalf of all who came to her and God and Jesus would hear her petitions. As a mediator of grace, Mary became an adored figure in the religious life of ordinary people. They flocked to her shrines, built chapels in her honor, and celebrated the special events in her life with festivals and processions.

Although they did not become official doctrines of the Catholic Church until the modern era, two important theological ideas about Mary had emerged by the twelfth century. One was that Mary had been taken up bodily or "assumed" into heaven at the time of her death. She existed, just like God the Father and the Son, in a heavenly realm where she could mediate for believers on earth. This doctrine of the assumption nurtured the image of Mary as the queen of heaven who reigned over the hosts of heaven at the right hand of Christ. Medieval art is resplendent with scenes of the Virgin with crown and jewels, displaying the signs of royal office.

The other idea about Mary evolved eventually into the doctrine of her immaculate conception. The church believed that although Mary was fully human and the product of sexual relations which passed on original sin,

God had cleansed her from this sin at the moment of her conception. God also preserved her from any additional sin during her lifetime. In this way she provided a pure, sinless womb for Jesus.

Mary and the Status of Women

What significance has Mary had for the status of women in the Christian community?[7] Her presence has certainly provided a feminine dimension in a tradition dominated by masculine symbolism for the divine. For many Christian women, Mary has also reinforced the idea that the virgin or chaste life is most pleasing in the eyes of God. This belief, as we have already seen, has had both a liberating and oppressive effect on women. Women as virgins did gain a measure of freedom and equality with men but only by learning to loathe their sexuality and female natures. But although Mary was a woman, the circumstances of her life could not be duplicated by ordinary women. The birth of Jesus was without pain, marriage was without the sexual union of two bodies, and death did not mean the decay of her flesh. After her death, Mary took on the role of queen with the exceptional honor and luxury that implied. Even when a more human vision of Mary developed in popular literature, it simply reinforced traditional ideas about women. In the popular stories, Mary polishes the ornaments in the temple, becomes hysterical at the crucifixion, and is soft-hearted rather than logical when dealing with sinful human beings. She deserves to be venerated because she was submissive and obedient. According to Marina Warner, there is a definite correlation between the popularity of Mary and the low status of women in past and contemporary cultures.[8]

WOMAN AS WITCH

Popular and Official Attitudes Toward Witchcraft

Toward the end of the fifteenth century in Europe, a detailed picture of the nature and activities of witches took form in the minds of church authorities, government officials, and ordinary people. At the heart of this image was the widespread belief that witches were people who had made pacts with the devil. They promised to worship the devil, be his sexual partner, and renounce the Christian faith. It was believed that, in exchange, witches gained the power to inflict harm on their neighbors through the practice of magic or sorcery. Witches were said to cause crop failure, illness, and even death. Particularly, it was believed that they had special powers over the procreation of children through their abilities to cause impotence, infertility, and abortion. Finally, many people believed that witches were able to fly through the air to attend group orgies where they worshiped the devil, ate the bodies and blood of children (mimicking the Christian Eucharist), and indulged their sexual appetites. At these orgies, as well as at home, it was said that the witches surrounded themselves with small animals or "familiars" which were really demons in disguise.

Historians generally believe that this picture of the witch existed only in the minds and writings of people and never in reality.[9] Throughout the Middle Ages, some village people did practice popular magic and healing, and fragments of Greek and Roman religious practices persisted in medieval Europe. These activities, however, were a far cry from the full-blown image of witch as it emerged in Christian history. The image of the witch was a product of folklore, ancient non-Christian religious traditions, and medieval Christian theology. People were accused of worshiping the devil and acquiring supernatural powers. They confessed—under torture—and thus a body of evidence accumulated that the church could use to crusade against witchcraft as a danger to the faith and the social order.

Up until the thirteenth century, the church in Europe had ambivalent feelings toward witchcraft. Some churchmen argued that since God alone controlled natural events, it was impossible for human beings to do so through magic and sorcery. Something that did not exist could not be punished. Others argued that the Bible itself recognized the powers available to some people through sorcery and communion with evil spirits (Exod. 22:18; Acts 13:6–12) and condemned it in the strongest terms. Some of the church fathers, including Augustine, took this position and penalties such as excommunication or long periods of penance were levied sporadically against witchcraft. In the thirteenth century, however, the church began to take a more uniformly harsh position. Witchcraft came to be associated with the worship of the devil and with various heretical groups which, it was commonly believed, promoted allegiance to the powers of darkness. Witchcraft became a crime of heinous proportions and the churches, both Catholic and Protestant, looked to the civil authorities to eliminate it through torture and executions. The result was the witch craze that spread throughout Europe and Great Britain and touched the American colonies as well. It did not abate until the eighteenth century.

The Association of Women with Witchcraft

Upon examining those individuals who were imprisoned and executed as witches, it becomes clear that women were much more frequently persecuted than men.[10] In some areas and periods, two women were executed for every man. In others, the ratios are as high as twenty to one or even one hundred to one. In Essex County, England, for example, 90 percent of the inhabitants tried for witchcraft were women. One historian indicates that the witch trials of 1585 left two villages with only one female each. Certainly in the popular imagination, the image of the witch was —and continues to be—female. Even our Halloween decorations and contemporary dictionary definitions reinforce the long-held belief that a witch is "a woman practicing usually black witchcraft."[11]

We can make several observations explaining why women were more frequently persecuted than men. The witch craze emerged in a period of violent sentiment against women as evil instruments of the devil. They were therefore likely candidates for devil-worship and pacts with the prince of darkness. The *Malleus Malleficarum* (which means "Hammer of Witches") was published in 1486 by two German churchmen as a guidebook for those who wished to rid the Christian world of witchcraft. Although other works echoed many of the ideas of the *Malleus*, it was the most popular publication of this kind. It specifically asserted that witchcraft was more likely to be found among women and it went on to give detailed reasons why this was so. (1) Women were by nature feebleminded and were easily swayed by false doctrines. (2) Women were also morally weak and were particularly inclined toward deceit and revenge. They would therefore not only be adept at keeping their activities secret, but they would seize any opportunity to cause harm to those around them. (3) The Christian faith of women was weak. They would easily renounce Christianity and have few qualms about stamping or excreting on the crucifix. (4) Above all, the *Malleus* insisted that women had insatiable lust which caused them to submit willingly to the sexual advances of the devil. They had, it was believed, "more pleasure and delight" with the incubus or demon who came to them in the night than with any mortal man. The identification of witch as woman was reinforced, of course, by the popular belief that the devil, as a divine power, had to be male when he assumed a human form.

Rosemary Radford Ruether has also observed that old women in particular were singled out for persecution as witches.[12] Reginald Scot, a sixteenth-century writer, describes the popular view of witches as "women which be commonly old, lame, bleare-eied [sic], pale, fowle [sic] and full of wrinkles. . . . "[13] This writer is echoed in the modern definition of the witch as an ugly old woman or hag.

Ruether and other scholars suggest some reasons why old women incurred such hostility.[14] In many medieval communities, it was the older woman who knew and passed on the folklore traditions regarding healing, abortions, and contraception. She was also the one to preside over births and she prepared corpses for burial. She knew how to prepare herbal medicines and how to use charms and spells to fight evil. These areas—birth, illness, and death—were believed to be the province of the witch. Furthermore, such women opened themselves to the hatred of others if their charms and medications were not successful.

The old woman living alone was vulnerable in other kinds of ways. Loneliness and poverty may have made her seem marginal or odd. The curses she might have muttered out of frustration were interpreted by her neighbors as spells and the summoning of evil spirits. In some ways, she may have made her neighbors, who were becoming increasingly concerned about their rights as individuals, feel guilty about their neglect of communal values and in turn take out their guilt on her. Also, she had few legal powers with which to defend herself against the machinery of church and state. Finally, it was believed that the devil physically marked his women and gave them special "teats" from which the demons could nurse. When exposed, the moles and growths common to an aging body sealed the fate of countless helpless women.

MEDIEVAL WOMEN IN PRAYER AND PROTEST

At all socioeconomic levels of society, women performed vital services and were often recognized for their contributions in everyday life. These circumstances alone challenged the official view of women as mentally and physically incompetent and as morally defective. Aristocratic women, for example, took full responsibility for running their husbands' estates while they were away at war or imprisoned. Women in the middle and lower classes frequently went out to work or did work at home in addition to child rearing and housekeeping. Some aided their husbands with a craft or business and frequently carried on alone after being widowed. Single women in urban areas ran their own businesses and there are numerous examples of single women who managed their own farms.

During this period the few women whose religious writings are known to us are largely silent about the roles they were assigned and the images with which they were described. There are, however, a few examples of clear-cut protest against the church's degradation of women and the culture's belief that a woman's main function was procreation. There are also more indirect challenges to the accepted status of medieval women in church and society from the pens and lives of some of Christianity's most revered saints—the female mystics of the thirteenth and fourteenth centuries.

Christine de Pisan

The fifteenth-century Frenchwoman Christine de Pisan was left a widow at the age of twenty-five and was able to earn a living through writing. She produced two popular prose works on women, one of which was a set of stories illustrating the virtues of women. She also wrote poetry in protest against the violent attacks on women by medieval churchmen and noblemen. Christine de Pisan argued that there was good evidence to show that many women were modest, gentle, and loving. As a group, they did not wage war and they did not oppress other people. Adam, she pointed out, was just as guilty as Eve in bringing sin into the world. What is more, she argued, women were the ones who remained faithful to Jesus during his trial and death.

Isotta Nogarola

Another woman of the same century, Isotta Nogarola of Verona in Italy, aspired to a life of academic scholarship. Although she acquired a wide knowledge of classical studies, including Latin, by the time she was eighteen, her efforts were not encouraged. Learned men failed to take her seriously, enemies accused her of sexual promiscuity and incest, and her female friends shunned and ridiculed her. Nogarola was forced to conclude that only the virgin life would give her the freedom and social approval she needed to pursue her studies. From 1441 until her death she lived virtually in seclusion on her own property. She studied and wrote on topics related to Christianity and she eventually gained praise from prominent men for her saintly and scholarly life. They could approve of an intellectual woman who had taken a vow of chastity, but not one who was marriageable or married.

One of Isotta Nogarola's surviving works deals with the question of Eve's responsibility for the origin of sin. She argues that Eve cannot be blamed for her partner's participation and that she was not even entirely responsible for her own actions. While Nogarola wished to protest against the excessive burden of guilt that the church had placed on Eve, she does this by accepting her own culture's definition of the nature of women: Eve could not be blamed because she was by nature weak and ignorant and was no match for the cunning serpent.

Margery Kempe

One of the few spiritual autobiographies extant from the medieval period was written by an Englishwoman, Margery Kempe. Kempe has left us an account of her answered prayers, visions, and prophetic insights which she believed to come from God in *The Book of Margery Kempe*. Her spiritual experiences persuaded her to alter her life style dramatically. After bearing fourteen children, she persuaded her husband to agree to a celibate marriage which she thought was God's will for her. She undertook a number of journeys to shrines and holy places including Santiago de Compostella in Portugal and the Holy Land. Margery Kempe aroused the anger of the clergy because of her flamboyant and eccentric behavior (she was prone to emotional outbursts and tears). Yet she was regarded with suspicion and hostility also because she believed that her spiritual experiences gave her the right to teach and advise, questionable activities for a medieval Christian wife.

Female Mystics

One of the pilgrimages Margery Kempe made was to a nun who lived alone in a room attached to the side of a church in Norwich, England. This nun was Julian, who, together with a number of other medieval women, made a significant contribution to the church's tradition of mystical theology which flourished in the thirteenth and fourteenth centuries. At the heart of the mystical tradition were the experiences of people who had acquired a direct and intimate knowledge of God in visions and at times of worship and meditation. Women frequently had mystical experiences which they then, on occasion, committed to writing. Julian of Norwich, for example, describes a series of visions or revelations that she received during an illness in her *Revelations of Divine Love*. Catherine of Siena writes about a similar set of experiences in *The Dialogue of St. Catherine of Siena*. Some of the nuns of the Cistercian monastery at Helfta in Germany also produced a large body of reports describing their visions and inner experiences.

The content of this mystical writing varies from woman to woman but there are certain common features. There is considerable emphasis on the physical suffering of Jesus and a free use of bridal imagery to describe the relationship between the Christian and Jesus. Both God and Jesus are also described in female and feminine images in some of the writings. One of the nuns at Helfta frequently referred to God as the mother of humanity to show that God's justice was tempered by love and comfort. Julian claimed that Jesus had the character and performed the activities of an earthly mother. Jesus sustained and loved the Christian and he gave the Christian life. He fed the Christian with his body just as a mother fed her child with milk. Julian also believed that, like a mother's love, the love of Jesus knew no end, even though he chastised the believer when necessary: "And though, possibly, an earthly mother may suffer her child to perish, our heavenly Mother Jesus can never suffer us who are his children to perish. For he is almighty, all-wisdom and all-love."[15]

The female mystics, apart from bringing a feminine dimension to the images used for God, represented an important avenue of power and self-affirmation for women in the Christian community. While they were excluded from offices within the structure of the medieval church, the mystics were regarded as figures of authority within the Christian community on the basis of their visions and intimate friendship with God. Catherine of Siena, for instance, was able to persuade the pope to move back to Rome from France because he believed that she had received authentic directions from God. One study by Caroline Bynum on the mystic nuns at Helfta stresses their role of authority among both men and women.[16] Although they held no official administrative positions, the nuns were sought out as spiritual advisers by lay men and women, the clergy, monks, and the other women at Helfta. The community believed, for example, that the mystics could provide information on the condition of people who had already died. Perhaps most significantly, the visions of women like Gertrude of Helfta sometimes enabled them to perform priestly duties like the forgiveness and absolution of sins. In her visions, Gertrude was told by God who had been forgiven and she was commanded to announce this absolution to the people involved. Also in their visions, the nuns were commissioned by God to serve others and to teach (often understood as preaching) what had been revealed to them. Those nuns who compiled the visions and life of Mechtild of Hackeborn described her in the following way: "She gave teaching with such abundance that such a one has never been seen in the monastery and we fear, alas, will never be seen again. The sisters gathered around her as around a preacher to hear the word of God."[17]

Medieval Christianity presents us with strong male voices praising the virgin but condemning women as women for their association with the flesh and sin. Yet it also has left to us, for the first time in Christian history, an array of female voices. Women write and their works endure. We hear direct and indirect protests against their status as they seek both to serve God and to develop their talents. We also have a picture of their conscious and unconscious efforts to circumvent some patriarchal limitations in order to find meaning and dignity in their lives. Within Catholic Christianity, the images of virgin and witch will continue to shape the status of women for centuries. The Protestant Reformation brings a new emphasis on women as obedient wives and devoted mothers, a shift that is explored in the next few sections.

CHAPTER 4

WOMEN IN AN ERA OF REFORMATION

Marriage

The church into which Martin Luther was born and ordained regarded marriage as a sacrament. As such, it was an indissoluble bond which allowed for the procreation and education of children and acted as a remedy for human lust. Celibacy, however, continued to be regarded as the more pleasing life style in the eyes of God.

Luther altered this medieval understanding of marriage and chastity. He removed marriage from its sacramental status yet simultaneously restored it as a relationship that was favored, and indeed commanded, by God. In the Protestant tradition, marriage rather than the celibate life became the norm or ideal for all Christians. As a result, the Reformation made a significant impact on the status of women in the domestic arena.[1]

Luther, as did numerous other Reformers inspired by his writings, used both theological and biblical grounds to defend his ideas on marriage. Luther rejected the church's idea that God laid down some laws that were binding on all Christians as well as "counsels of perfection" that were intended to be kept only by a small elite in the Christian community. The church taught that people who lived according to the more rigorous laws would earn greater rewards in heaven. Virginity and the ascetic life were seen as examples of these counsels of perfection.

In objecting to this concept, Luther made two important points. First, he argued that God did not lay down two sets of laws for humanity but expected the same obedience from everyone. Second, Luther argued that no human being could ever earn grace from God through obedience to laws. God's grace and salvation were bestowed as gifts upon those who trusted

61

in the righteousness of Christ. Doing good works, performing religious ceremonies, and denying oneself physical pleasures had no bearing on a person's salvation.

Both Luther and Calvin, and a host of other reformers, also argued that marriage was preferable to celibacy on biblical grounds. God had commanded Adam and Eve to be fruitful and multiply. Man and woman were made for the purpose of sexual union according to God's design. They should feel joy and not guilt in their natural inclinations (although Calvin did caution against overindulgence). The reformers looked for inspiration particularly to the pastoral epistles which see marriage as normal and desirable and also to the stories of the patriarchs of the Old Testament in which God blesses marital union. The reformers did agree that for a very few Christians who were born without sexual desires, the celibate life was appropriate. These Christians had been given exceptional gifts, however, and they ought not denigrate marriage.

The doctrines of the Lutheran and Calvinist Reformation did not lose sight of medieval ideas on the nature of marriage. They described it as a satisfactory means of procreation and as an acceptable way to deal with human lust. In many writings marriage was recommended as a way to curb the pervasive fornication to which monks, nuns, and priests were said to be driven. In much Reformed literature, however, emphasis was given also to marriage as a spiritual relationship between a man and a woman. Marriage was an arrangement of reciprocal trust and caring. It was characterized by a sharing of duties and it was said to reflect the highest form of love known to human beings, the love of God. The Reformers also describe marriage as a union that both the man *and* the woman were to choose freely.

The honor accorded to marriage in both Lutheran and Calvinist circles had an impact upon the status of women. Since sexuality was no longer viewed as evil, the married woman, at least, was not cast in the role of temptress and seducer. She was seen as fulfilling part of God's design and not as working against God to corrupt the minds and bodies of men.

Since the Reformers removed marriage from its sacramental status, divorce became a possibility. The medieval church could only allow for the separation of husband and wife, not their divorce, since it was impossible to dissolve the sacramental bonds of marriage. While the Reformed churchmen and the Protestant civil authorities were reluctant to approve of divorces, they acknowledged that in some instances (usually adultery and desertion) such a measure was appropriate. Martin Bucer in Strasbourg even went so far as to extend the grounds for divorce from adultery to spiritual incompatibility. In Geneva, John Calvin insisted that women as well as men be permitted to initiate divorce proceedings.

In giving practical shape to their doctrines, the Lutheran and Calvinist Reformers entered into marriages themselves and urged other celibate Christians to do the same. Priests serving the newly formed reformed congregations were encouraged by take wives. The marriage of clergymen affected the status of women in two ways. For some women, it meant a legitimization of a relationship in which they were already involved. It was not uncommon for priests to live with women as mistresses for long periods of time, fathering their children and providing a livelihood for them. Such women, however, were without respect in the community and neither they nor their children had any claim on the priest's estate at the time of his death. Marriage gave these women legal status and rights as well as security and respect.

A married clergy in both Lutheran and Calvinist circles also meant a new sphere of activity and power for some women as "ministers' wives." As we will shortly discover, the Protestant home became an important center for teaching the gospel and passing on the Christian faith. Within this community of families, the minister's home acquired a preeminent status. Although many modern Christians have difficulty associating the role of the minister's wife with liberation, the sixteenth century provides examples of just such a situation. Women who married Lutheran or Calvinist ministers often found themselves presiding over households that were the centers of cultural and intellectual activities. They offered hospitality to theologians, advice to other clergy, and bed and board to young students. Luther's wife, Katherine von Bora, presided over barnyard, fishpond, orchard, a host of servants, children, sick visitors, student boarders, and church leaders and theologians in their huge Augustinian cloister, which had forty rooms on the first floor alone. Katherine Zell, wife of Strasbourg pastor Matthew Zell, summarized at the end of her life some of the work she had carried out: "I honored, cherished and sheltered many great, learned men, with care, work and expense. . . . I listened to their conversation and preaching, I read their books and their letters and they were glad to receive mine."[2]

The Good Woman as Wife and Mother

Reformed Views on Domestic Life. Women, as we have seen, were not denounced as seducers and corrupters in the Lutheran and Calvinist literature and they were not treated with scorn and derision. Calvin objected to the vulgar expression that women were "a necessary evil" while Luther took a stand against those who "despised the female sex." Men and women had the same potential for sin and the same opportunity for redemption. They were called by God, however, to different vocations. Women pleased the Creator by caring for the home, bearing children, and accepting the rule of men in all spheres of life.

For Martin Luther, the subordination of women was the result of woman's sin. Before this divine punishment, male and female were equal in their responsibilities and privileges. Calvin, however, interpreted the Genesis stories through the eyes of Paul in some of his commentaries (but not in his important *Institutes of the Christian Religion*). Calvin argued that woman was created in subjection to man since she was made as his "helper" and since she was made *after* him and *for* him. This original subjection was simply aggravated by her sin. The outcome was that women throughout history were not permitted to exercise authority over men but instead had to be obedient to them. This obedience of course precluded teaching in public or assuming positions of government. Luther, too, stressed subordination, saying that a woman had to take her husband's name and follow him to his place of residence to show her obedience. She was permitted to disobey her husband only when his commands caused her to disobey God. The reformers stressed that the husband was not to oppress his wife with cruelty. If this did occur, however, a woman had to be submissive. She could desert her spouse only if her life was in serious danger.

Luther and Calvin both removed the virgin life of the monastery as an option for women, thus restricting their roles to those of motherhood and homemaking. They elevated these tasks, however, to the status of a "vocation" ordained by God. The church had previously restricted its understanding of vocation to believers who entered religious orders or the priesthood. The reformers insisted, in contrast, that the jobs performed by all baptized Christians were vocations. Women were given the tasks of bearing and rearing children, managing households, and caring for their husbands. These were described to Protestant women as "glorious and enobling works" which were pleasing in the eyes of God and equal in value and dignity to all other human endeavors.

The role women were to fulfill at home was also enhanced by the Lutheran and Calvinist emphasis on the family as the "school of faith." It was at home that children learned the Bible, the catechism, and basic reformed doctrines. Mothers as well as fathers were responsible for imparting the reformed faith. They were to act, in the words of Luther, as "apostles and bishops" to their children. Calvin claimed that both mother and father were to "rule" their children. He described the mother as setting the pattern for future generations through the instruction and influence of her sons. She was the parent who had time to hear Bible and catechism lessons and who could most easily supervise family worship.

The Protestant Reformation also affected the status of women outside the home. All Christians, it was said, must learn to read the Bible as the authoritative guide to faith and practice. Luther therefore called upon the civil authorities in Germany to establish schools for young girls and boys. In the Reformation city of Geneva, both girls and boys were sent to school to learn reading, writing, arithmetic, and the catechism. Although some of the secular writers of the Renaissance had also stressed the intellectual capabilities of women and recommended their education, the Reformation further advanced the general improvement of education for both women and men.

Women in the Life of the Church. On the basis of their belief that the Bible commanded the subordination of women to men, the Lutherans and Calvinists did not allow women to preach, be ordained, or participate in the governing bodies of the churches. Luther's reasons went beyond the Bible. The preacher needed "a good voice, good eloquence, a good memory, and other natural gifts."[3] He did concede that in very unusual circumstances, when no men were available, a woman might preach as a temporary substitute. Also, both the Lutherans and the Church of England continued the Catholic practice of allowing midwives to baptize babies on the verge of death. Calvin, however, strongly objected to this practice on the basis of his ideas about baptism and the administration of the sacraments. He cites several church councils and follows the line of the theologian Tertullian who stated that women could not baptize or assume any priestly function. Yet both Luther and Calvin express ideas about the ministry and church organization that could have been used to support the full participation of women in the new Reformed congregations.[4]

Luther, for example, confidently asserted the doctrine of the priesthood of all believers. By this he meant that all Christians had the responsibility of carrying out certain priestly duties. They were obligated to pray to God on behalf of other believers and to speak the gospel to each other. Luther believed that some Christians should be ordained to preach and to administer the sacraments in a public ministry. Yet when it came to the important duties of prayer and proclamation, both the clergy and the laity had equal responsibilities. The laity included both men and women.

In Calvin's commentary on 1 Corinthians and in the *Institutes*, he provides insights that could have resulted in a new role for women in the churches.[5] Calvin argued that, unlike doctrine, matters of human governance such as church polity and forms of worship could change according to the expectations of a particular culture. The church had to be sensitive to what was regarded as "proper" and "decorous" in certain circumstances.

Calvin included the silence of women in church as a matter of human governance.

The Virgin Mary

The image of Mary, theological symbol and object of devotion, faded from the beliefs and piety of the Reformed churches. One reason for this, of course, was the emphasis in Calvin and Luther on marriage rather than on the celibate life. With the decline of the religious orders the image of Mary as the pure virgin lost much of its original significance as a prototype for the life of chastity. Also, the Lutherans and Calvinists emphasized the Bible as the sole authority for faith and practice. They could not find enough about Mary in the New Testament to continue the popular cult that had grown up around her over centuries of Christian history.

CATHOLIC WOMEN IN AN ERA OF REFORM

During the sixteenth and early seventeenth centuries, the Catholic Church experienced a period of revival and reform. The changes that occurred were in part a reaction to Luther and the spread of Protestantism and in part the result of reforming impulses already at work within Catholicism. This movement in Catholicism is referred to by historians as the Counter-Reformation.

The Establishment of New Religious Orders

One aspect of the Counter-Reformation was a series of efforts to establish new types of religious orders for Catholic women. Included in these new orders were the Ursulines, founded by Angela Merici, and the Institute of the Blessed Virgin (the Ladies of Loretto in the United States), founded by Mary Ward. These new orders were conservative in that their founders retained the virgin life as essential to a life dedicated to God and insisted on a pattern of firm obedience to the male spiritual directors associated with the orders. Yet these women also tried to introduce some radical innovations into Catholic sisterhood.

The new orders were established with the goal of serving other people through nursing, education, and care for the poor. This goal had important effects on the organization of the groups. The women who joined were permitted to be out in society. They were required to spend less time reciting prayers and Daily Offices, which normally occupied the time of the nun. The women wore plain, everyday clothing instead of the traditional habit and if they lived together in a community their life was much less structured than was generally true with cloistered convents. The vows they took were not binding for life but were "reversible."

These innovative groups met with considerable opposition. The Catholic Church was fearful that virgin women in the world would be a source of scandal. The Catholic hierarchy was convinced that the Protestant Reformers would be quick to use any kind of immorality on the part of the clergy or nuns against the church. The assumption that virgin women were likely to seduce and corrupt celibate men still prevailed. The lengthy council held at Trent reiterated with force the earlier decrees that women living in religious orders should be cloistered in communities, shut off from the world, and strictly disciplined.

Additional opposition to the new orders was based largely on financial considerations. It was argued, for example, that without wealthy patrons and long-held tracts of land, these groups could not survive financially. Also, since the women did not take solemn vows binding for life, they could take whatever property or money they had brought to the order with them if they left. The church could not count on inheriting the wealth originally placed at its disposal.

Most of the new orders eventually succumbed to the opposition and dropped many of their innovative features. A cloistered life style and solemn, binding vows were reinstituted. Some of the women did retain their commitment to education by taking in students as boarders to be taught within the convents. Also, the Daughters of Charity did succeed in getting official approval for much of their original plan with some concessions. They were able to proceed with their hospital service by agreeing to go outside their house in pairs and by agreeing to wear the traditional habit. The innovative features of the other orders were only slowly allowed to reappear in the nineteenth and twentieth centuries. Despite their eventual repression, however, the new orders provided significant role models of women who were involved publicly in the duties of teaching, nursing, and social work. These tasks were important steps taking women beyond the confines of home and cloister.[6]

Women in Defense of Catholicism

Some historians recently have given attention to the question of how Catholic women, particularly those in convents, reacted to the spread of Lutheranism and Calvinism. Jane Dempsey Douglass describes the experiences of one woman, Sister Jeanne de Jussie, who lived in Geneva during the growth and triumph of Calvinism.[7]

Jeanne de Jussie's writings emphasize the point that Catholic women were much more loyal to their faith than Catholic men. She describes how women endured beatings, broken families, and verbal abuse because they would not accept Protestant ideas. She also writes about the support of some high-ranking Catholic women for her convent. These women of status and wealth came to the aid of the sisters when they were harassed by Protestant men and when their convent was ransacked. The account of Jeanne de Jussie confirms stories from many other regions in Europe which describe how many Catholic sisters strongly resisted the closure of their convents and the disbanding of their orders. Not only did they object to the Protestant understanding of the Eucharist, but they saw the Protestant glorification of marriage as a form of constraint on women.

Jeanne de Jussie's account of the behavior of the Calvinist women in Geneva also shows that they too were active in the spread of reformed doctrine and worship. She writes, for example, about the Calvinist women who worked at their spinning and weaving in full public view on Catholic holy days. She also claims that these women were quick to annoy others with their "preaching." The wife of an apothecary "meddled in preaching" and visited the convent to praise marriage, denounce chastity, and irritate the nuns. Jeanne de Jussie adds an interesting note: This woman was regarded by the Calvinist leaders as illumined by God to teach and preach divine truth, an attitude which contrasts sharply with some of their own words on appropriate roles for women.

PROTESTANT WOMEN ACTIVE IN REFORM

The activities described by Jeanne de Jussie were carried on by many other women as the Reformation spread throughout Europe. So far as historians can tell, women did not serve as ordained clergy in the Lutheran and Calvinist churches nor did they contribute to the written body of reformed theology. Yet they conducted a whole range of activities that supported and spread the ideals of Luther and Calvin. They wrote and sometimes published letters advocating Protestant principles. They circulated books containing reformed doctrine and they sometimes sponsored the publication of such material. They visited influential people to win them over to the cause of the Reformation and, on occasion, conducted church services when clergymen were either absent or unwilling.

Katherine Zell

Katherine Zell married a priest with the knowledge that both she and her husband would be subjected to extreme disapproval for abandoning the celibate life. When her husband was denounced by the Bishop of Strasbourg, Katherine took up her pen in his defense. In an open letter to the bishop, she attacked the age-old practice of clerical celibacy. She accused the bishop of being concerned only with his own pocket since he could no longer tax the priests who were living with mistresses. Marriage, Katherine claimed, would actually save souls since priests with natural sexual desires would not have to commit the sin of fornication. As she bordered on discussing matters of doctrine in her letter, Zell felt that she had to defend her "unwomanly" behavior. She turned to the Bible for support. "You remind me . . . that the Apostle Paul told women to be silent in church. I would remind you of the word of this same apostle that in Christ there is no longer male nor female and of the prophecy of Joel: 'I will pour forth my spirit upon all flesh and your sons and your *daughters* will prophesy.'"[8]

Katherine Zell was dedicated to the cause of reform. In addition to her defense of clerical marriage, she wrote a preface to and published a collection of hymns to enhance congregational participation in the new churches. She also devoted herself to caring for the sick and the imprisoned in Strasbourg as well as the multitudes of refugees who flocked to the city to escape religious warfare.

Argula von Grumbach

The Bavarian noblewoman Argula von Grumbach is also representative of the numerous women who furthered Lutheranism and Calvinism. She wrote to the University of Inglostadt, protesting the dismissal of a young faculty member because of his Lutheran sympathies. She defended her action by saying that she was driven to speak out because no man was willing to do so: "I send you not a woman's rantings, but the Word of God. I write as a member of the Church of Christ against which the gates of hell shall not prevail, as they will against the Church of Rome."[9] She was imprisoned twice for her support of Luther and particularly aroused the hostility of the church authorities by conducting reformed worship services in her home and by conducting funerals without authorization.

French Noblewomen

A group of noblewomen were very influential in the spread of Calvinism in France throughout the sixteenth century. Despite the hostility that they encountered in many places, the women persuaded others to join the Calvinist party and instructed people who were interested in the ideas of the Reformers. Calvinist schools were established for teaching young children, as well as an academy for the training of clergy modeled on Calvin's school in Geneva. These Frenchwomen sponsored public debates and seminars to air Protestant and Catholic views. Perhaps most significant was the protection they offered to Calvinist believers in a country where the Reformation was never welcomed and often actively persecuted. The women gave refuge and support to young Calvinist women fleeing from Catholic families and to reform leaders fleeing from Catholic authorities. Calvinist congregations were allowed to flourish on land owned by these women and protected by their private armed guards.

PROTESTANT WOMEN OUTSIDE THE MAINSTREAM

Character of Radical Protestantism

In several places throughout Europe the Lutheran and Calvinist churches gained the support of powerful political leaders. As a result they became "established" or "national" churches. The civil authorities enforced the doctrine and worship of the reformed churches and supported them in material ways as well. The churches, for their part, upheld the prevailing social values and political structures. The membership of the church was virtually identified with the citizens of a particular state or territory.

In the sixteenth and seventeenth centuries a number of groups appeared which accepted many of the ideas of Luther and Calvin but which rejected any close alliance between the church and the political establishment. Some of these groups, such as the Amish and Mennonites, emerged on the continent of Europe while the Quakers and Baptists were shaped by English Puritanism. They differed greatly on theological issues and on matters of life style but they did share some common characteristics: they believed that the church should include in its membership only those people who could show clear evidence that they had received God's saving grace. They believed that individual congregations should govern their own affairs. They stressed that all regenerated Christians were equal in God's eyes and could therefore act as God's representatives on earth. A theologically educated and ordained ministry therefore was given little emphasis. Many of these groups also believed that the Holy Spirit, through visions and direct revelations, guided Christians in matters of faith and practice. Some groups placed a strong emphasis on the Bible as an authoritative guide, although they acknowledged the importance of the Spirit as well. A corollary of this last feature was the high value placed on freedom of conscience in matters of religion.

The groups were opposed with vigor not only by the Catholic Church but also by the Lutherans and Calvinists as well as the Church of England.

Their emphasis on direct inspiration and individual freedom was seen as a threat to the order of society that Christianity traditionally upheld. One concrete way in which this threat was believed to manifest itself was in the public role women assumed (and were sometimes given) in the movements. Certainly they appear in some of these traditions in more varied roles than in either Lutheranism or Calvinism, and they were numerically prominent, often making up over one-half of a congregation's members. Opponents often used the fact that the groups were composed chiefly of the "weaker sex" as a point of derision.

Views on Marriage

Most of the written works from this cluster of traditions come from the pens of its male leaders. Descriptions of the marriage relationship and the role of women in the church repeat traditional ideas on silence and subordination. The German Anabaptist preacher Balthasar Hubmaier turns to the old dichotomy between body and spirit to stress the carnal and hence evil nature of women. The biblical tradition is used to show that woman was created as man's helper and inferior. Obedience to husbands in the home and men in society is the most frequent counsel.

The writers and their female followers, however, sometimes break away from traditional patterns of thought and action. They occasionally stress that a wife had a right to freedom of conscience in religion and a right to worship as she saw fit. Some writers even urged women to desert their husbands if they hindered their faith, and they added religious incompatibility to adultery and desertion as grounds for divorce. The godly had to be separated from the ungodly.

Women in the Congregations of
Radical Protestantism

In order to be faithful to the practices of the New Testament church, some groups revived the office of deacon for women who wished to do charitable work. This occurred, for example, in some Mennonite churches in the Netherlands and in North Germany. The office, however, was merged with that of the widow and was restricted to women who were over sixty and whose husbands had died. They were not ordained to this office but in some places were called "church officers."

When the groups outside the Protestant mainstream vested authority in the individual congregation and when they claimed that all who had been saved were spiritual equals, they had to confront the possibility of female participation in the government of the congregation. Most leaders were reluctant to give a real voice to women. A few, such as the English Separatist John Smyth, proposed that women have a vote in the selection of a pastor, the excommunication of disobedient members, and other affairs of the congregation. Other leaders permitted women to speak on issues but did not grant them a vote. The Quakers, discussed in the next chapter, gave women the widest opportunities to govern their congregations.

Opinion also varied on whether or not women should preach or prophesy. Many Reformers took the prohibitions of Timothy as the final word, yet they worked within a theological framework that said that the Holy Spirit could inspire any believer directly, sidestepping the learned and the ordained. Lay preaching in fact was a prominent feature of these movements. Historian Joyce Irwin has observed that although the leaders may not have approved of women preaching, their theology left the door ajar.[10]

Women, with and without official approval, did exercise a preaching ministry among some congregations. Often their preaching was decorous and popular. In one General Baptist congregation in London, for example, hundreds of people gathered on Tuesday afternoons to hear women lecture on spiritual matters. Women preached among the Baptists in the Netherlands and in the cities of Salisbury, Kent, and Ely in England. The Swiss Anabaptist Frena Bumenin, who sat nude while waiting to give birth to the Antichrist, may have gained greater notoriety but in so doing discredited female preaching.

In light of the scarcity of written material by women, it is difficult to come to any conclusion about the motivations of those who preached. Some probably were seeking attention. Most seemed to believe clearly that they had a message from God to communicate and a right to do so. It may be that underlying their determination was a sense of frustration with the limited roles of wife and mother and with exclusion from the political arena.

Lasting Effects

Some of the groups outside the Lutheran and Calvinist mainstream simply disappeared while others grew, prospered, and became institutionalized. As they acquired structure, they tried to conform their beliefs and practices to those of the established churches, seeking tolerance and acceptance from a world they once rejected. The silence and subordination of women in the home and church were upheld with vigor and the activities of women were curtailed.

A few movements found an atmosphere of religious toleration and opportunities for growth in the American colonies, particularly in Pennsylvania. One such group was the Ephrata Community (originally German Dunkers), which settled in Lancaster, Pennsylvania. The community stressed withdrawal from the world, rejection of a state or national church, individual conversion, and a direct knowledge of God through mystical experiences. In some ways, it also anticipated features of American groups in the nineteenth century that encouraged the participation of women. Conrad Biessel, leader of the community, spoke of a divine female principle, Sophia, as well as the male principle, God. At Ephrata celibate women lived together in one building, sharing the household work with each other but not doing the chores for men. In addition to spinning and quilting, the women developed artistic and musical skills by practicing calligraphy and singing.

Did the Reformation of Calvin and Luther enhance or diminish the status of women in the Christian community? Women were not given opportunities to teach, preach, or govern the reformed congregations and they lost the monastery as a sphere of female power and autonomy. Yet the theology of the Reformation terminated the second-class status of marriage and the association of women with evil because of their reproductive functions. In some places it also brought educational opportunities for women, created divorce laws in their favor, and brought reformed Christians at least to the theoretical threshold of full female participation with the doctrine of the priesthood of all believers.

When we look at the actual activities of women during the era of the Reformation, it is possible to detect certain themes that will appear again as we trace the status of women in American religious history. Women frequently found channels for meaningful participation and dignity despite limitations imposed on them, as did Katherine Zell and the French Protestant noblewomen. Also, women tended to be given and assume wider roles in groups that flourished outside of or in opposition to the culturally dominant churches and emphasized the direct action of the Holy Spirit in human lives.

CHAPTER 5

WOMEN AND CHRISTIANITY IN THE AMERICAN COLONIES

MODIFIED PATRIARCHY

Most of what we know about colonial views on the nature of women and appropriate behavior for them in the church comes from the writings and sermons of Puritan ministers from New England. The Puritans not only wrote and published a great deal of material, but their works were sold and read throughout the colonies. In this way, they played an important role in shaping the character of American religious life, especially in its white Protestant expression. The records of individual congregations from the southern and middle colonies as well as New England supplement these more formal sources. The church records give us some idea of whether or not the theories regarding the role of women were carried out in a practical way, and whether or not women found opportunities to act contrary to these ideals.

What we lack is satisfactory knowledge of how women viewed themselves within the context of the Christian community. Some written works of colonial women, either once left uncatalogued or regarded as "anonymous" by many libraries, are being discovered slowly. They are shedding light on how women responded to their situations in both thought and action. What emerges from all of these sources is not the expected picture of colonial churches as uniformly and rigidly patriarchal. Women are certainly treated and viewed as subordinate to men, yet the religious communities of the colonies reveal active women and a surprising appreciation for the feminine.

The Weaker Sex

In the early decades of the colonial settlements (1630s to 1650s) the ancient image of "the bad woman" so prominent in medieval thought and

75

witchcraft lingered on, especially in New England. The minds of women were thought to be incapable of handling anything more than basic learning. Poet Anne Bradstreet had to beg a hearing for her work in 1671 from he who "says my hand a needle better fits."[1] Learning for women was not only inappropriate and futile, but also dangerous. Governor John Winthrop was convinced that the wife of Mr. John Hopkins of Connecticut had lost her sanity "by occasion of her giving herself wholly to reading and writing" and by meddling in things proper to men.[2]

In a society that valued religious and moral integrity above all else, the accusation that women were spiritually and morally "weak" was even more serious. Women were regarded as easy prey for sexual seduction and as powerful seducers. It was said that they were prone to lying and more susceptible to doctrinal error and heretical opinions. Woman as the "Devil's dunghill" was an image not entirely out of line with much of colonial thought. Although it was disputed by many, the idea that a woman did not even possess a soul was discussed in colonial literature. The traditional images of Eve and Jezebel informed this view of the gullible woman who had direct contact with the powerful forces of darkness.

The appropriate response to such weakness was to keep women under control or in subjection in all areas of life. Throughout England's new colonies, the ideal wife was described as submissive and obedient to her husband. She yielded to his preferences rather than her own and she devoted her life to his service. As minister John Robinson pointed out, in a harmonious marriage one spouse would lead and the other would follow. Both nature and the Bible left no doubt about who would be the follower. Women were excluded also from positions of leadership in public life. Although they fared better legally than their English sisters and did cast the occasional vote in New England town meetings, colonial women generally could not vote or hold public office.

Subjection was enforced in the churches of the colonies as well. Church membership was open to women in all of the colonial denominations and women were expected to attend worship regularly. The office of minister was closed to them in the Anglican and Puritan traditions, but the Quakers, as we will see, allowed women a remarkable degree of participation as ministers and missionaries. Women generally did not vote in congregational meetings to call a minister or to discipline a member. They were also discouraged from speaking in such meetings. There are records of congregations that even forbade women to sing in the worship service and of churches in which women were seated apart from the men. In Puritan congregations, all candidates for church membership were in theory required to give a public declaration of their conversion. However, some ministers insisted that women only speak privately about their conversions for fear that they would violate the New Testament command of silence. Finally, women were thought to be incapable of theological study or discussion and were required to defer to male church members or their husbands in matters of belief.

Exceptions to the Rule of Silence and Subjection

There are exceptions, however, to this patriarchal rule which begins to emerge less than a generation after the first Massachusetts settlement. These exceptions grow stronger as the colonial period progresses. Women, for example, did find some opportunities for power and influence in the colonial churches. In the southern colonies women are recorded as liberal benefactors in the records of many congregations. Mistress Blake, for example, provided for the interior decorations of the Anglican church at Charles Town, and Catherine Besouth furnished some of the silver plate in the prestigious Bruton Parish Church in Williamsburg.

The records of Wenham Church in Massachusetts reveal a congregation open to the participation of women and women who were prepared to take full advantage of this liberality even in the 1640s. The congregation continued to insist that women give a full, articulate, and public account of their conversion experiences. When a married couple left the congregation, the wife was given her own letter of dismission. The congregational records show that one woman, Joan White, publicly spoke for this privilege and many other issues. She took an active role in governing the church and it appears that her ideas were acted upon.

Another exception to the patriarchal norms with which American religious life began was the development of a more positive image of women in New England at the end of the seventeenth century. The concept of spiritual and moral equality between men and women began to replace the image of woman as inclined to false beliefs and sin. Despite their hostility toward the Roman Catholic veneration of Mary, some Puritan clergy began to use the mother of Jesus as a positive counterpart to Eve, the seductive temptress. The prominent New England minister Cotton Mather wrote, "As a woman had the Disgrace to go first in that horrid and woeful transgression of our first Parents, . . . so a Woman had the Glory of bringing into the World that Second Adam, who is the Father of all our Happiness."[3] Even Eve was given some positive features: The curses of subordination and painful childbirth which she brought on women had given them added incentives to turn to the consolations of Christianity in this life. Women therefore gradually came to be regarded as the spiritual and moral equals of men. They shared the same sinful nature, had the same opportunities for salvation, and faced the same obstacles to faith in everyday life. In John Bunyan's popular allegory of the Puritan life, *The Pilgrim's Progress*, Christiana, Pilgrim's wife, makes an identical but less celebrated journey to the celestial city.

Environmental factors in colonial society probably played some part in this shift in thinking. Cotton Mather led the way in the transition. He, like his colleagues, had to deal with the fact that his congregation was made up of more women than men. The admission of new female members generally began to exceed that of males in the 1660s, and by the early part of the eighteenth century, there were two women for every one man in many congregations.

Women throughout the colonies provided essential services to the growing new settlements. Their economic roles in farm and plantation households put them in positions of practical equality with male family members. Although the subordination commanded in the Genesis story continued to be the spoken ideal, the Galatians emphasis on equality was closer to the truth in many colonial homes.

Puritan views on the nature and role of women were also shaped by the theological framework of the Reformation. The Reformers' emphasis on the goodness of marriage and their praise for women as devoted wives and mothers tended to mitigate the long-standing belief that the female nature was inclined to evil and more radically separated from the grace of God.

The fruits of conversion for men and women in New England also overlapped significantly by the early eighteenth century. Funeral sermons and other clerical treatises do not contain specific definitions of feminine virtues as distinct from masculine. Such distinctions later emerge as a formidable influence on women as America moved into the nineteenth century. A century earlier, however, women as "new creatures in Christ" were encouraged to take up the same kinds of pious activities as their male counterparts.

Of particular interest are the outpourings of admiration for women who lived out their faith by reading, writing, and talking to other people about the things of God. Women in the clerical families of Benjamin Colman and Cotton Mather were encouraged to read the Bible as well as other devotional books and works on church history and theology. Colman's daughter, Jane, studied theology systematically. Mather presented all the women who had cared for his wife during her final illness with a book as a token of his gratitude. He taught his daughters shorthand so that they could take notes on sermons and, as did many other Puritan ministers, he encouraged women to write for the cause of salvation. Sermon notes, private thoughts on Bible passages, and daily diaries often stayed within the privacy of a woman's home. On occasion, however, the written works of women were published by their admiring pastors or quoted in sermons before an entire congregation.

A virtuous woman, like a pious man, was also praised for conversing on religious subjects. Religious conversation sometimes extended beyond immediate family to groups of female neighbors who gathered together to discuss the Christian faith. Mather writes approvingly of one such group of women who met in 1706 to pray and discuss their religious experiences. Benjamin Wadsworth likewise praised Bridget Usher for promoting pious and "savoury" conversation.

A third variation in the patriarchal pattern of colonial religion was the Puritan conception of marriage, a product of the Protestant Reformation and English ecclesiastical thought. The model of dominant husband and submissive wife received some modification. So also did the prominent belief that marriage was nothing more than an approved channel for the satisfaction of male lust and the procreation of children. The Puritans increasingly came to place more emphasis on the elements of love, trust, and mutuality and less on subjection. Spouses were commonly referred to as friends, partners, and companions. The English Puritan John Milton, author of *Paradise Lost*, even argued that when these elements were not present, a true marriage did not exist. Certainly New England began to echo phrases such as "delight in each other's eyes" and "the desire of thine eyes" when they spoke of marriage in the early 1700s. No Puritan denied, however, that the husband was the head of the household and the wife his subordinate.

The elevation of marriage to a relationship of some spiritual depth had an interesting counterpart in the way the relationship between God and human beings was expressed in Puritan piety, especially after 1690. Marriage was used as a popular analogy for the way in which God and the Christian were joined. Both were loving unions between sovereign and subordinate parties. Marriage brought duties and privileges to a wife just as salvation brought duties and privileges to a believer. The Christian, like the ideal wife, was to avoid anything that would arouse Christ's anger. The Christian was to observe Christ's rules and be loyal and pure in the relationship. In turn, Christ would behave like a loving husband toward his good wife. Women, as passive brides and obedient wives, became role models for all Christians. In this way they acquired a new community status.[4] Ministers encouraged their congregations to learn humility and receptiveness from the women in their midst.

By the end of the eighteenth century, views on the nature of women and their place in American society and churches had again shifted. The Puritan inclination to see male and female as spiritual equals leading similar lives of devotion was altered. It became increasingly common to believe that women were endowed by nature with a whole cluster of characteristics that could be identified as distinctly "feminine." These natural attributes defined the "sphere" or area of activity in which women would be happy and competent. Women, for example, were said to be frail, emotional, intuitive, and nurturing. It was also believed that women were naturally more religious and moral than men, something the Puritans would have been quick to refute. Religion and morality along with child rearing therefore were defined as part of the female sphere. While this shift in attitude represents more restrictions and repression in some ways, it also represents a new phase of female influence within the Christian community.

ANNE HUTCHINSON, THE "AMERICAN JEZEBEL"

The story of Anne Hutchinson and the religious community in Massachusetts Bay reveals some of the themes we have been discussing so far. It involves the deep-seated suspicion that women were easily influenced by false beliefs and that they had tremendous power over other people in spreading those beliefs. It involves the existence of female gatherings in New England for a discussion of the Sunday sermon and for Bible reading. It also involves the radical equality that some women discovered in the Christian gospel and that was hinted at in the agrarian Puritan household.

Hutchinson was born into the family of Francis Marbury, a clergyman highly critical of the Church of England, in which he had been ordained. Page Smith has interpreted Hutchinson's later conflict with the New England authorities as the inevitable outcome of a special father-daughter relationship nurtured by the Protestant Reformation.[5] The Reformation placed in the father's hands a responsibility for teaching all members of the household to read and think about the Bible as the source of salvation. Hutchinson acquired these academic skills from her father. She developed them by attending faithfully the church of the English Puritan John Cotton. She took notes on Cotton's sermons and gradually acquired a theological education through her own initiative.

When she was twenty-one, she married William Hutchinson and began an unremarkable period of childbearing and rearing. She also engaged in the practices of nursing and midwifery. Her husband, a merchant of some success, was described by Governor John Winthrop as "a man of very mild temper and weak parts, and wholly guided by his wife."[6] These words probably reflect anger at the fact that he remained loyal to his wife through her eventual excommunication and banishment.

In 1634 the Hutchinson family followed Cotton to Massachusetts Bay, where he became the minister of a church in the expanding settlement of Boston. The house they built was directly across from that of Governor Winthrop. Anne Hutchinson maintained her keen interest in Cotton's theology and began to invite a group of women to her home to read the text on which the Sunday sermon was based and then to review the main points of Cotton's presentation. Her activity was at first praised as behavior appropriate for a pious woman, but she was soon accused of heading a movement that threatened the peace and well-being of the entire Bay Colony.

Although he later denied it, Cotton's theology had tendencies toward Antinomianism, which was attracting a growing number of followers in New England. "Antinomian" means "against the law" and refers to the belief that those who have been redeemed by Jesus no longer need to observe civil, moral, or church laws. The "New England Way," however, was based on obedience to such laws. The New England clergy reconciled this legalism with salvation by grace by saying that obedience was a necessary preparation for the coming of grace and an inevitable sign that conversion had indeed taken place. Any denial of this was a deliberate weakening of the social fabric.

Hutchinson was viewed in Massachusetts as one of the chief perpetrators of Antinomianism. She denied that she advocated a total freedom from laws for Christians, but she did interpret John Cotton's sermons in such a way as to disturb deeply the Massachusetts settlement. She claimed that grace was an intensely personal experience between God and the individual. To say that good behavior had to precede or follow that experience was to return to salvation by works. More importantly, she claimed that the Holy Spirit who dwelled in the redeemed person would directly guide that person as to what to believe and how to behave. Thus, there was no need for magistrates or clergymen to preside in an authoritative way over the community.

The ministers and magistrates were troubled by the implications of Hutchinson's teachings. They moved against a number of men who they believed to be Antinomian sympathizers, banishing or disenfranchising them. Hutchinson, however, provoked a particular outburst of wrath not only because of her doctrinal ideas but because she was a woman. Her accusers were fearful of her power to seduce men with her false doctrines and to spread them among gullible women at her weekly meetings. Also, her theology suggested a new kind of social order for the Christian community which would be free of oppressive restrictions on human behavior. This new order without doubt would have allowed a high degree of freedom and participation to women. Hutchinson was already a concrete example of what might occur if Massachusetts took salvation by grace alone seriously. She was demonstrating the consequences to which the Bay Colony authorities feared Antinomianism would lead.

The clergy responded initially by passing a resolution prohibiting Hutchinson from holding any more meetings in her home. This clerical gathering was followed by two trials, one by the civil magistrates and one by the church. In the trials the issue of Hutchinson's sex was brought up repeatedly. She was formally accused of disturbing the peace by holding meetings in her home, "a thing not tolerable nor comely in the sight of God nor fitting for your sex."' She was chided for acting more like a husband than a wife and for neglecting her family and encouraging other women to do the same.

Hutchinson showed herself to be a formidable debater and able theologian in the course of her trial. She used the Bible in her defense, pointing out that the New Testament specifically approved of older women teaching and counseling younger women at home. She also turned to precedents for women preaching in the history of the church, particularly mentioning a woman from the Isle of Ely in England.

In the spring of 1638, Hutchinson was both excommunicated from the congregation in Boston and banished from the colony. Already well into another pregnancy, she moved with her family to Rhode Island, where they enjoyed an atmosphere more tolerant of religious diversity. The Massachusetts clergy and magistrates convinced themselves that Hutchinson had repeated the ancient pattern of woman consorting with Satan and then infecting those around her with evil. In the excommunication decree she was "delivered up to Satan" and the news that she had given birth to a badly deformed and dead fetus was seen as the final proof of her spiritual condition. This conclusion was further confirmed when it was learned that Mary Dyer, one of Hutchinson's supporters, had also delivered a premature and dead fetus. Hutchinson had acted as midwife at the birth, which John Winthrop described in salacious, albeit secondhand, detail. Hutchinson's death at the hands of Mohegans in 1643 was viewed as God's final punishment.

One notable aspect of Hutchinson's life in New England is the large number of women who found meaning in her teachings and who surrounded her with a community of support. Some of her followers were certainly attracted by her skills in folk medicine and midwifery, but it is possible that many were also attracted to her new perspective on the social order.[8] Were these women consciously trying to acquire more rights and a wider role for themselves in Massachusetts society? Were they drawn to Hutchinson unconsciously or intuitively out of deep but unspoken frustrations with their lot in life? These questions are matters of debate and speculation. Hutchinson, however, remains the first well-known woman on the North American continent to raise questions about the appropriate status of women in church and society.

We also must note the fact that Hutchinson was only one of a number of women in New England who tried to participate in the reformulation of Puritan doctrine and who were prosecuted for failing to comply with clerical authority. In many cases they showed a spirit of independent judgment on the basis of a direct revelation from God. Anne Eaton of New Haven, for example, was excommunicated six years after Hutchinson for refusing to acknowledge the validity of infant baptism. Lady Deborah Moody was forced to flee to Long Island for similar opinions and Mary Oliver was deported to England for questioning the conversion experience as a requirement for church membership. Any impact that women might have had on the development of Puritan doctrine was finally curtailed by the increasing inclination to try rebellious and activist women as witches in New England.

THE REVIVAL TRADITION

In the early years of the eighteenth century the Protestant churches in the American colonies and Great Britain experienced a period of apathy. Membership obligations were not taken seriously, sermons were academic presentations on good living, and deeply-felt piety was missing from the general understanding of Christian life. This tendency was reversed in a period of general religious awakening in both countries. The conversion or rebirth experience became the hallmark of the Christian experience, as did devotion to righteous living. Preaching changed in style and content. It became more emotional and less formal in an effort to awaken congregations to their sinfulness and to encourage them to turn to Jesus for salvation. This particular approach to Christianity is described by historians as evangelicalism.

In the American colonies, the First Great Awakening began with outbreaks of conversions in New England and New Jersey. In the 1740s the Awakening spread throughout the colonies as a result of the itinerant preaching of the evangelist George Whitefield. The fervor and emotional enthusiasm generated especially by the itinerant preachers troubled many

ministers who feared the disruption of church order. One way to dispar-
age revival preaching was to describe it as a "species of insanity" to which
women were particularly susceptible. Yet the clergymen who believed
these allegations did not know their facts. The period of the Awakening
provided one of the few phases in American history during which new
male members in the churches exceeded new female members.

Despite the attraction that a new emphasis on sin and salvation held
for men, the Awakening was also significant for women in the colonial
churches. In this evangelical style of Christianity, women found additional
and wider opportunities for participation in the Christian community.
The conversion experience itself, for example, became a public ritual in
which women were encouraged to join. John Wesley, an important evangelical leader in England and the founder of Methodism, appointed
women as group or "class" leaders and welcomed their public speaking as
it took the forms of prayer, personal testimony, exhortation, and exposi-
tion on religious literature. Eventually he gave his approval to Sarah Mal-
let, Mary Fletcher, and other women who wished to engage in "biblical
exegesis and application" or preaching. Before the end of the eighteenth
century, the Free Will Baptists permitted women to serve as preachers and
evangelists. Among these women was Mary Savage, who began to preach
in New Hampshire in 1791. Also, there were other ways of nurturing and
participating in the revival of Christianity, as the stories of Anne Dutton,
Selina, the Countess of Huntingdon, and Sarah Osborn show below.

The character of evangelical Christianity in the eighteenth century provides us with some clues as to why women were acquiring a wider role.
For one thing, the evangelicals emphasized the experience of conversion
which dramatically transformed both women and men. All people who
had experienced grace were compelled by God to tell others about it. Authority to speak or write was rooted in God's "warming of the heart" and
not in theological education or church approval. Also, many of the evangelical leaders were open to experimentation when it came to matters of
church life. If the experiments brought more people to Jesus, then they
were acceptable. As an experiment, Wesley permitted laymen to preach
and it was not long before laywomen were included. He believed that the
evangelical awakening signaled extraordinary times in which exceptions to
the biblical command of silence could be made.

Anne Dutton, Writer

Only fragmentary evidence from a wide variety of sources makes up the
knowledge we have of the English evangelical Anne Dutton. She was a
prolific and talented writer who nurtured the distant American awakening

through her letters, poems, and tracts. Her family evidently had sympathy with the emotional piety of British evangelicalism and they exposed her to ministers of the same persuasion. Benjamin Dutton, her second husband, was a Baptist pastor in the same circles in Huntingdonshire, England. Anne Dutton was greatly impressed by the evangelical call to a devout and holy life, and she strongly desired to do some "service in the cause of Christ."[9] She was discouraged, however, by her disabilities (both real and imagined) as a woman and determined simply to serve her husband as efficiently and cheerfully as possible.

In 1747 Benjamin Dutton lost his life at sea while returning from a trip to the American colonies. Anne Dutton, who had already established herself as a serious religious writer, devoted herself to a lifetime of religious activity. She carried on a massive correspondence with converts to evangelical Christianity "in divers parts" but particularly in America. She corresponded with George Whitefield and their relationship became one of mutual respect and support. Whitefield encouraged her to increase her correspondence as a service to new converts, particularly to those in South Carolina.

Dutton, however, did not confine her writing to correspondence but also published numerous poems and tracts and edited a periodical entitled *The Spiritual Magazine*. All of her writing was infused with a sense of wonder at the transformation God had carried out in her own life and a sense of obligation to open this experience to others. She believed that writing was a divine vocation to which she was called. God was using her as an amanuensis. She had no difficulties therefore in overcoming the opinion of some that women should not write on religious topics. God had called her to "feed His lambs." She often wrote anonymously, not out of modesty or shame, but to make certain that her work was published.

In addition, Dutton did not hesitate to speak out against those ministers who deviated from her understanding of the gospel. Of her growing dissatisfaction with one minister she wrote, "I thought it was my Duty to acquaint him with it; and accordingly did it after having sought the Lord about it."[10] Nor was she afraid to usurp the role of pastor in offering counsel and advice to a host of correspondents regarding their religious obligations. Her experience of God's grace gave her a confidence in her worth and destiny which society could not shake.

Another Englishwoman, Selina Hastings, the Countess of Huntingdon, also had an impact on revivalism in the American colonies. She is usually noted for her generous gifts of money to further the work of Wesley and Whitefield. Yet she pioneered women's work in missions and in social reform organizations. She organized a mission to the Cherokee people of

Georgia which she directed from a distance. Her relationship with Whitefield and Wesley was characterized by equality and mutual counsel.

Sarah Osborn, Teacher

Women's groups for Bible study, prayer, and discussion proliferated in
New England as a result of the First Great Awakening. Jonathan Edwards,
one of the leaders of the Awakening, advised young female converts who
were seeking direction to join such a group. Shortly after the visit of
Whitefield to Newport, Rhode Island, in 1741, a number of women "who
were awakened to a concern for their souls" proposed to Sarah Osborn
that she form a society with them to meet once a week. The women established a set of rules for each member to sign. They collected money for
firewood used during meetings and decided on who was to be admitted as
a new member. The group flourished throughout Osborn's lifetime and
gave a substantial donation to an African mission project in 1774. Her experience with the Newport society encouraged Osborn to take an active
role in the revivals that swept the area in 1766–67.

We know about Osborn's religious activities in Newport because they
have been celebrated in a biography of her by her pastor, Samuel Hopkins.
An addition of great value to this material, however, is a collection of
Osborn's correspondence with a friend, Rev. Joseph Fish, which has been
published by Mary Beth Norton.[11] Here we do not see a woman of ideal
piety as defined by a clergyman who believed himself superior, but a
woman struggling to defend the work she believed God set for her and to
understand the criticism she was receiving from people around her.

Osborn's years as a young woman in Newport were riddled with trag-
edy. She lost her first husband at sea in 1733 after only a short marriage
and the birth of a son. She operated a school to support herself and her
child until she married Henry Osborn, a successful businessman. When
her husband's business failed and he became disabled a few months after
their wedding, Osborn was again forced to turn to teaching to support her
new family. Although women frequently adopted this method of earning
money, they did not escape criticism for working "out of their sphere"
even before their sphere was carefully defined. Osborn's letters testify to
this. She was particularly troubled by the charge that she was neglecting
her family by teaching. She admitted that "some things Might be done
with more Exactness than now," but she had female friends she could call
on for help and the income was vital to her family's well-being.[12]

Her correspondence reveals that in 1765 a group of free black people
were meeting in her home on Tuesday evenings and a group of slaves on
Sundays. The sessions involved singing, reading, and "plain familiar con-

versing" about spiritual matters. Word of her compassion for people spread rapidly in Newport and white people, children and adults, males and females, began crowding into her home on other evenings during the week. In January 1767 the number had reached an extraordinary 525 people in one week.

Her letter to Fish reveals that he as well as others in the community advised her to give up her activities because she was not qualified to take on a leadership role, because she was stepping dangerously close to forbidden territory by holding discussions with both men and women, and because she was threatening the social order by making black people proud and disobedient (presumably because the gospel preached equality). Osborn responded to all of these concerns.

She claimed, first, that she did not seek out a public role for herself but that God had thrust it upon her. She asserted that she had tried to get help from the male leaders in the churches, but they were reluctant to get involved. Also, the people of the community preferred Osborn's counsel to that of men. She also claimed that her message was not intended to instill pride in people but instead to give them the internal resources to be faithful and obedient. Finally, she made an observation that would be echoed by countless other women who saw themselves as integral parts of the Christian community. She found purpose, refreshment, and strength in her evening meetings which simply could not be supplied by the more "feminine" activities that Fish had recommended.

Sarah Edwards

Evangelical Christianity claimed that conversion had to be followed by a life totally consecrated to God. Conversion meant that a person's priorities in life had to be reordered, placing God first. For women, this sometimes meant that God's call had to be obeyed, even when it took them beyond what society regarded as "proper" for a woman. Both Anne Dutton and Sarah Osborn had this experience. Sarah Edwards's rebirth gave her a similar kind of power. She was freed by her allegiance to Christ from always having to seek approval from other people. In 1742, Edwards, the wife of theologian and preacher Jonathan Edwards, had an intense, extraordinary experience of religious emotion which lasted for nine days. She described her feelings as those of peace and exultation which had physical manifestations in periods of fainting, vigorous conversation, and even rising up and leaping with joy. She claimed that she felt swallowed up in the light and beauty of Christ, that she swam in the rays of Christ's love "like the motes swimming in the beams of the sun."[13]

Edwards came to an important realization as a result of her experience of religious ecstasy. God's estimate of her life became the only judgment that mattered. She was freed from the obligation to meet other people's standards, including those of her neighbors and her husband, for a virtuous wife. Her happiness, she claimed, rested entirely in a source that would not disappoint. She had participated in the beauty and love of God and it had "deepened her self-awareness and offered her a freedom and independence that was new, enjoyable and worthy of celebration."[14]

Black Women and the First Great Awakening

The preaching of evangelists such as George Whitefield was also met with enthusiasm by black women, slave and free, in the eighteenth century. White colonists were initially reluctant to seek black conversions since they feared that a Christian servant could not be held in bondage. Legislation denying this, however, soon became common in the colonies. Where Christianity was introduced through efforts such as those of the Church of England's Society for the Propagation of the Gospel, black women were converts. Their conversions to Christianity increased with the First Great Awakening.

Motivated by the transforming power of revival Christianity, many black women participated creatively in the life of the Christian community. The slave Phillis Wheatley, for example, wrote poems and letters on the strength she found in Christianity and an elegy for George Whitefield. Katherine Ferguson organized the first Sabbath school for children in New York City. She was concerned that poor, orphaned children learn to read and write even though she did not have these skills herself. She also sought ways to care for poverty-stricken and lonely unwed mothers. A sense of mission also motivated the women of Richard Allen's African Methodist Episcopal Church to serve as nurses during the epidemic of yellow fever in the city of Philadelphia.

QUAKER WOMEN

In 1646 George Fox had a profound religious experience which he felt compelled to communicate. He preached throughout England, gathering around him a nucleus of followers which would eventually become the Society of Friends or Quakers. The new religious movement was attractive to women from its beginning. Elizabeth Hooten became one of the first Quaker converts and one of its earliest preachers. She eventually traveled as a missionary to the West Indies and the American colonies. Margaret Fell opened her home as a meeting place for the Quakers, wrote on behalf of the movement, and served as its financial secretary. It is not difficult to determine the features of Quakerism that appealed to women in both Britain and America. Claims about the equal spiritual status of men and women were given concrete form in domestic life and in the public arena, particularly in the institutional structures of the Society. In addition, the Quaker religious experience provided women with a source of power with which to criticize cultures in which injustice and intolerance flourished.

One of the distinctive beliefs of Quakerism was that of the Inner Light which existed within each person. Salvation came to those who cooperated with and followed the leading of the Inner Light. Since this direct call from God came to all people, the differences recognized by society between rich and poor, learned and unlearned, male and female became irrelevant among the Quakers. A tangible expression of this Quaker belief was the refusal of the Society to use any deferential titles even for monarchs, magistrates, and bishops. Equality of status within the group was also carried out in the interaction between men and women. New forms of the wedding ceremony replaced the traditional phrase "love, honor, and obey" with words reflecting Quaker mutuality. George Fox, even in his position of leadership, did not hesitate to accept counsel and advice from women.

The equalizing influence of the Inner Light, however, had its most radical effects on the religious activities in which women were permitted to engage. Local Quaker groups met together weekly for worship, which was followed by a business meeting. Early in Quaker history separate Women's Meetings were formed which were generally equal in scope and status to those of the men. Women's Meetings, for example, began in Virginia in 1672, in Pennsylvania in 1681, and in Maryland before 1700. The women collected and disbursed their own money for charity, disciplined members, discussed topics such as the proposed marriages of members and appropriate female dress, and elected delegates to larger, regional gatherings of Quaker women.

Even more noteworthy, however, was the Quaker practice of opening the preaching ministry to women as well as men. The Quakers eliminated the need for a specially trained interpreter of the Bible by claiming that each believer would be led to the truth by the Inner Light. They also eliminated the sacraments as part of worship and therefore eliminated the need to set someone apart to celebrate them. They did not formally ordain people to the ministry. In the weekly Quaker meeting, silence was observed until a member, male or female, felt led by the Spirit to speak. The Quakers did "acknowledge" certain members, again male or female, as being gifted with preaching and counseling skills and they charged these individuals with spreading the Quaker message and instructing and overseeing the Quaker communities.

The Quakers were criticized for their openness to the preaching ministry of women. George Fox, and later Margaret Fell in her pamphlet "Women's Speaking Justified, Proved and Allowed of by the Scriptures," were compelled to defend the practice. They made three important points related to the Bible. (1) They believed that men and women were equal in status before the Fall in Genesis and were restored to that equality by the redemptive work of Jesus. (2) They also claimed that the words in Corinthians prohibiting the speaking of women were addressed to a specific group of people who had not experienced God's grace. (3) Finally, both Fox and Fell pointed to numerous women who spoke and taught on religious matters. Mary, for example, was the first to declare that Jesus had risen and Mary, the mother of Jesus, declared her faith in the Magnificat. The way in which Fell and Fox approached the biblical material was informed by their belief that the Inner Light was always illuminating the Bible in new ways. Traditional interpretations of certain material could be altered drastically under the guidance of the Spirit.

Women preachers played a significant part in the spread of Quakerism from England to New England and throughout the American colonies. They received financial support from local societies as well as certificates stating the soundness of their beliefs and the permission of their husbands. Male missionaries carried similar statements of release from their wives. Leaving a family in the hands of her husband, Patience Brayton, for example, journeyed from Rhode Island to preach in the middle and southern colonies. Jane Hoskins is recorded as preaching in New England as well as Ireland and Barbados. Sophia Hume, after the death of her husband, became an active itinerant preacher in the southern colonies in the eighteenth century and wrote a number of tracts and sermons for publication. Upon her departure to London to do missionary work, the Charles Town Society of Friends placed this tribute in their minutes: "This Day our Antient [sic] and Worthy Friend Sophia Hume sailed from hence. . . . We are sensibly convinced that nothing less could induce her to this Service but the strongest persuasion of her Love and Duty to Mankind, in becoming an Instrument in Publishing the Glad Tidings of the Gospel of Life and Salvation by Jesus Christ."[15]

As is clear from the words on Sophia Hume, the Inner Light was a source of strength and power for many Quaker women. They undertook journeys that called for enormous physical endurance. They also defied established authorities who opposed Quakerism by preaching in forbidden towns and territories. Mary Tompkins and Alice Ambrose were pilloried, whipped, and expelled from Virginia, and Mary Dyer, one of Hutchinson's most faithful supporters, was hanged in Boston in 1660. Dyer refused to cooperate with attempts to get her to stay away from Boston and to get her execution reprieved. It seems that the profound experience of the Inner Light enabled some Quaker women to make autonomous decisions about their life's work even when they were hard pressed with family responsibilities. When they were not preaching these women assumed traditional roles of homemaker and mother without questioning them. When God called, however, they answered despite pregnancy, young children, and the needs of husbands.

Because of the initiative of many women and the attitudes of some men, colonial American religion does not present us with a monolithic picture of silence and subordination. A handful of seventeenth-century Puritan women as well as eighteenth-century evangelicals and Quakers were compelled by the experience of conversion to move beyond prescribed roles and self-understandings. Colonial clergymen also began to replace the image of woman as inherently evil with the idea that men and women are equally inclined to sin and possess equal opportunities for redemption. This change in attitude was extended even further in the nineteenth century as the "cult of true womanhood" evolved.

CHAPTER 6

WOMEN ORGANIZING
FOR MISSION AND REFORM

THE CULT OF TRUE WOMANHOOD

By the middle of the nineteenth century in America, a cluster of ideas on the nature of women and their appropriate role was firmly planted in the popular mind of white America. These ideas make up what historians have called the "cult of true womanhood" or the "cult of domesticity."[1] The word "cult" is used to indicate that this was an almost sacred ideal to which many people were devoted. The ideal American woman was described as submissive, morally pure, and pious. She found power and happiness at home in the role of wife and mother.

The cult of true womanhood permeated American culture even in remote corners of the frontier. It spread mainly through the publishing industry which expanded and flourished between 1820 and 1850. The nature and role of women was a prominent topic in women's magazines such as *Godey's Lady's Book*, in novels, and in religious literature.

Domestic

Domesticity was an essential feature of the ideal woman. Her sphere was the home where she reigned as a queen over a kingdom. It was carefully distinguished from the male world of politics and business. In most literature, woman's sphere was described as complementary to man's and different from it, not as inferior. The male sphere was a competitive scene of brutal economic and intellectual struggle. In contrast, woman was to make the home a place of stability and calm, a refuge from the outside world. Her tasks were ones of nurturing and support. She was to comfort and cheer her husband, raise her children, manage the housework, and care for the sick. What little time was left over could be devoted appropriately to needlework, flower arranging, letter writing, and the reading of inspiring literature.

This separation of spheres had roots in American economic history. For much of the colonial period, women played a major role in the production of food, clothing, and household articles such as soap and candles in the home. These products were often supplemented by custom-made items from local craftsmen who also worked at home. A growth in population, the expansion of transportation, and advances in technology, however, began to change this situation. People with money to invest promoted schemes to produce large quantities of products economically and efficiently by focusing the efforts of a person or group of people on one particular product. Some of this specialized production initially took place in homes, but it gradually moved out of the household and into factories. The rewards for work became wages and profits. Farms also became mechanized and began to specialize in large quantities of certain crops which were exchanged for cash. These changes were accompanied by a growth in areas such as banking and insurance. Business and manufacturing therefore became the sphere away from home which was dominated by men. Although some women became factory and farm workers, many others were left in the home with the economically unproductive tasks of child rearing and housework.

The belief that men and women had different spheres in life was reinforced by ideas on the nature of women that were circulated in popular literature. Men and women were said to be endowed by nature with different character traits. Women were more affectionate and emotional as well as less rational. Women were prone to physical and mental illness. Perhaps most significantly, many nineteenth-century works claimed that women were naturally endowed with an inclination toward moral righteousness and religion.

Virtuous and Pious

Nineteenth-century America reversed the traditional view of woman as prone to sin in the image of Eve. Women were seen not as morally and spiritually inferior to men, but as superior. They were idealized as paragons of virtue and piety while men were cast in the role of sensual beasts who constantly assaulted female morality. The traditional Christian fear that the lust of woman was insatiable was reversed by the belief that woman was less carnal and sexual than man.

Because of her moral purity, the true woman was given formidable tasks in safeguarding the social order of the new American republic. Through quiet persuasion and diligent example, she was to tame the wild nature of husband and sons and make them into good citizens. She was to throw a "light of purity" upon the naughty world of men. If a woman's virtue was compromised, the results were portrayed in Victorian literature as calamitous. A woman's moral function was so important to society that she was threatened with death and mental illness if she took liberties with her sexuality.

Closely related to the belief in woman's moral superiority and the separation of male and female spheres was the century's glorification of motherhood. Fathers interacted less and less with children as they worked away from home. Many women were left with the responsibility of raising children, which developed into a semisacred vocation and an important source of power. This may have been society's way of compensating women for their diminished economic role.[2] Certainly the glorification of motherhood was influenced by the educational psychology of the time, which claimed that early influences on a child determined that child's later character. Victorian culture gave mothers the task of passing on religion and morality to future generations. The nation, and indeed the progress of civilization, could not do without them.

Nineteenth-century America not only viewed women as morally superior to men but also as spiritually superior. Religion therefore became an integral part of the domestic sphere over which women were to reign. They were "peculiarly susceptible" to the Christian message. Ministers suggested that women were by nature meek, imaginative, sensitive, and emotional, all qualities that were increasingly coming to be associated with Christian piety. They added that women more readily responded to Christianity out of gratitude for the way in which this faith had elevated their social status. Women were viewed as imitators of Christ. Like Christ, they brought redemption to the world through their moral virtue and religious fervor. Like Christ, they endured the sufferings of this life with patience and in silence.

The ideas on women and religion in the cult of true womanhood were recognizing in theory what was already true in fact. Religion was increasingly being abandoned by some men seeking political power and economic well-being. Women were left to teach the Bible to their children, oversee family prayers, and enforce church attendance. Women themselves also filled the pews and, as we shall see, supported the charitable, mission, and reform movements that the churches sponsored. It is even possible to interpret the identification of women with religion as a way of dealing with conflicting values.[3] Some men pursued wealth and prestige, often in very non-Christian ways, yet they continued to profess belief in the importance of traditional moral and religious values. They may have quieted their consciences by assigning to women those areas of life that they held dear but treated lightly.

Along with being domestic, religious, and moral, America's ideal woman was submissive. She was passive, weak, dependent, and in a state of perpetual childhood. She was to exercise her influence behind the scenes, always deferring to the authority of husband in the home. Submission was treated as ordained by God; to flout it was to throw the order of the universe into confusion. In many nineteenth-century novels, the qualities of willfulness and independence belong to the world of white men, while white women, children, and black people are celebrated for their submission and the moral power that comes from this. Very little attention, however, was given to the dilemma this created: If women were morally and spiritually superior, why should they be obedient to men?

Effects of the Cult of True Womanhood

This picture of the true woman became an ideal for American women in all economic classes but could become a reality only for middle- and upper-class women living in settled communities. Did this ideal benefit or degrade women who tried to shape their lives according to it? The cult of domesticity did present a formidable obstacle to political, economic, and occupational advancement for women. It also required them to erase their sexuality in order to acquire spiritual and moral status. Yet women did gain some important advantages, some of which were particularly relevant to their status in the Christian community.

First, educational opportunities beyond the elementary level began to open up for women to give them training in household management and child rearing. Second, the identification of women and religion led some clergymen to reshape Christian beliefs in ways that would be more pleasing to women.[4] Thus, the doctrine of infant damnation was abandoned. Hymns stressed the themes of Christ's love and God's mercy and pastor Henry Ward Beecher spoke of the maternal love of God which never wavered. Jesus was increasingly interpreted as one who loved his enemies and who sacrificed himself for others. Finally, women acquired a sense of self-worth and an impetus to action from the constant assertion that they were morally and spiritually superior to men. They were prompted to ask why they should not take a greater part in running the world since they were really only a "little lower than the angels."

ORGANIZING FOR CHARITY AND REFORM

A second period of revival swept the United States during the early decades of the nineteenth century. Preachers emphasized that conversion had to result in good works and, after 1800, this meant participation in the work of the many voluntary groups which were springing up. Clergy and laity alike joined to channel the religious enthusiasm of the revivals into associations designed to create a Christian America.

Women were swept into the revival fervor, outnumbering men as new converts to Christianity. Encouraged by their pastors and the groups already formed by evangelical women in Great Britain, American women joined a multitude of female voluntary societies between 1800 and 1850. For the most part, the societies were for religious, benevolent, or reform purposes, or they were concerned with the care and rearing of children. The cult of true womanhood gave women the right and power to extend morality and religion throughout America, as long as they were deferential to male authority. Also, as industrialization expanded, a growing number of women had the leisure time to pursue voluntary work.

Maternal Societies

The maternal societies, which were concerned with the tasks of motherhood, were local groups which have left few official records. It was common in some parts of the country, however, for Christian women to meet weekly to pray, discuss books on child rearing, and share their experiences as mothers. The members of the Maternal Association of Dorchester, Massachusetts, "determined to form ourselves into an association for prayer" in order to ask for guidance in discerning "the proper time and manner of administering reproof, correction and instruction in righteousness."[5] These groups were in some measure a response to the glorification of motherhood. Women who participated and who left records of their experiences clearly believed that they had a duty to teach their children religion and morality and the power to shape the future of the nation.

Missionary Societies

Many of the voluntary societies in America were motivated by a strong desire to bring the Christian faith to large segments of the population in the "godless" cities or on the "barbaric" frontier. Again, women were prominent participants. They usually worked to raise funds to support a variety of efforts such as missionaries to Native Americans, Sabbath schools to teach reading and religion, and the distribution of tracts and Bibles. The Female Domestic Missionary Society for the Poor of the City of New York, for example, promoted Sabbath schools, distributed Bibles, and aided churches in poor sections of the city. Sometimes their efforts went toward helping young men get through seminary or toward paying for preachers to minister to seamen. Money was often collected from the members' own weekly savings in "cent societies" or came from the sale of sewing and knitting. Many of these female groups became affiliated with national societies such as the American Bible Society.

Benevolent Associations

The care of the sick and the poor, especially in the cities, became the responsibility of women's benevolent groups. Often led by women of wealth and status in the community, these groups accumulated and controlled vast sums of money from legacies, bazaars, and solicited contributions. The benevolent groups cared for orphaned children, indigent young women, and widows. They provided food and clothing and, in some places, shelter. Some groups opened schools which taught reading, writing, arithmetic, needlework, and religion. A Female Humane Association was founded in Baltimore to help poor women and run a charity school, while similar organizations emerged in New York and Philadelphia. These women anticipated modern social work not only in their belief that education was a way out of poverty, but also in their use of "lady visitors" who called on women in the slums to teach them child care and housekeeping skills.

Reform Associations

Another type of female society, the reform society, emerged in the 1820s and 1830s. The reform groups directed their attention to the creation of a Christian America through social change rather than through individual conversions alone. Many of these groups were touched by the nineteenth-century hope that a perfect society, the kingdom of God on earth, was within reach.

Women took part in reform groups concerned with peace, temperance, and prison reform. One of their most significant efforts, however, was their work in moral reform. Inspired by the waves of revivals which swept the northeastern states in the 1830s, women in New York and Boston resolved to close the cities' brothels and convert the prostitutes. Their attack on prostitution was overshadowed, however, by the double sexual standard of society. Society condemned and ostracized the prostitute, but her male customers were excused. In contrast, the reformers believed that male sensuality and manipulation had caused the fall of their sisters in the first place. If guilt was to be assigned, it should fall more upon the men than the women.

The moral reform groups spread from the cities throughout New England and New York. They adopted bold tactics in running their organizations and in accomplishing their goals. Members as well as the societies' male missionaries descended upon brothels to pray with and talk to the prostitutes. They aided parents in seeking runaway daughters. One woman masqueraded as a laundress in order to gain admittance to a brothel suspected of hiding a runaway. In its crusade to eliminate the double standard, the movement used its newspaper to urge women to shun men in their communities who were suspected of sexual promiscuity. The names of men known to visit brothels were published along with the names of suspicious employment agencies. Finally, the movement used women as traveling missionaries to organize auxiliaries and soon adopted a policy of hiring only female employees. Women edited the journal as early as 1836 and also did the bookkeeping.

Effects on the Status of Women

What gains can be charted from all this activity?[6] The support of women was vital to the spread of Christianity in the last century throughout the United States. Women contributed great sums of money and countless hours to the religious and social welfare of many citizens. Their services in bettering the living conditions of people in urban areas met a need that neither government nor business was prepared to consider. In addition, the female associations encouraged and deepened loyalty to and knowledge of the democratic process of government. The voluntary societies, however, were also channels through which women themselves made some gains. The societies provided women with approved ways of participation in church and society as well as opportunities for self-development and companionship which broke through the isolating barriers of the domestic sphere.

The voluntary groups gave women a chance to use their physical and mental resources outside the home. They emerged at a time when educational opportunities were restricted and when women were being eased out of the few occupations (such as midwifery) they had followed in colonial society. What is important for us to note is that women were encouraged to join these groups by ministers who preached on the "right" of women to work for others. Most clergymen not only believed that women were suited by nature for charity, but they also stressed that such groups were simply extensions of a woman's role as mother and guardian of morality and religion. Women were welcomed as helpers in the task of Christianizing America, especially since men's interest in religion was diminishing. Women, however, had to stay as helpers. They were to assist the men, doing their work modestly and in subtle and quiet ways. Most of the women in the voluntary groups accepted the idea of "woman's place" yet they decided to take full responsibility for their sphere with a vengeance. As reformer Lydia Maria Child observed, the clergy had changed the household utensil into a living, energetic being and they had no spell to turn it into a broom again.[7]

The voluntary groups also gave women an opportunity to learn certain organizational skills which enhanced their own sense of self-confidence and self-worth. They served as group officers, they published appeals and advertised their cause to the public, they learned to conduct business meetings, and they collected and disbursed large sums of money.

Finally, women benefited from the support of other women which they experienced in reform and religious groups. Even when burdened with family and household responsibilities, women provide us with evidence that they made group meetings a priority. They learned from each other. They shared joys, sorrows, and concerns. They acquired a sense of solidarity with other women. For many, the missionary society or the "cent society" was a "chief source of enjoyment."

Organized Feminism, Women's Rights, and the Christian Community

We can point to a variety of factors in American society that help to explain the rise of feminism and the women's rights movement in the 1830s and 1840s. Many women who were at home guarding morality and consuming manufactured products felt increasingly useless in a society that valued work for wages and profits. Women became more aware of their political and legal disabilities as more and more men participated widely in the democratic process. Also, as more women received secondary education, they increasingly became frustrated by finding that many professions and institutions of higher learning were closed to them.

Did the religious climate of America in the middle of the century contribute to the emergence of feminism?[8] The answer is probably a qualified yes. Through the Protestant societies, women acquired the right to associate and to work (albeit voluntarily) outside the home. The praise that was heaped upon them for doing so could not help but have contributed to their feelings of pride and confidence. The sense of solidarity with other women, essential to feminism, was also nourished by the societies. Women not only identified with the members of their groups but sought reforms on behalf of other women and against the activities of men. Temperance groups spoke out against the drunk husband who victimized his wife, moral reform groups against the male lecher who victimized the young woman, and benevolent societies against the factory owner who took advantage of his female employees. Yet most women did not question the idea of separate spheres or even the appropriateness of male authoritarianism. Only a small number of women actually moved from the religious associations to groups that asserted the political, economic, and social rights of women based on their common humanity with men.

Antislavery Roots of the
Women's Rights Movement

A direct link between revival-grounded reform and feminism can be found by examining the antislavery societies of the 1830s. The campaign to abolish slavery in part grew out of the revival preaching of Charles Finney and his followers. The male antislavery societies, which flourished, were complemented between 1833 and 1838 by the growth of over one hundred female societies. To nineteenth-century America, it was not unexpected that the cause of slaves would commend itself to the sensitive and compassionate nature of women. Some women responded with enthusiasm and, as in other reform movements, they expressed particular outrage at the treatment of black women who were sexually exploited and separated from their families. Unlike the other reform groups, however, the antislavery movement raised directly the issue of the status of all women.

In joining in arguments against the defenders of slavery, women were led to reflect upon their own situation in American society. The abolitionists argued that all human beings had a right to life, liberty, and happiness, and some women observed that they were a glaring omission. The abolitionists quoted Gal. 3:28 on behalf of the slaves, and some women began to realize that they, too, were included in the biblical promise of equality. The more some women thought about their own status, the more similarities they could see with that of the black slave. White women and free black women also had little power or liberty and they were treated simply as a means to promote the welfare of men. A cry for freedom for the slave therefore was coupled with a call for the liberty of women.

However, the practices of certain women in the antislavery movement, rather than theories, acted as the strongest catalyst for the emergence of the women's rights movement. Sarah and Angelina Grimké, both eloquent speakers with a firsthand knowledge of the conditions of slavery, began to speak to "promiscuous" audiences made up of men and women. Lucretia Mott and Elizabeth Cady Stanton asked to be received and seated with the official male delegates to the World Antislavery Convention in London. And a host of women circulated petitions door-to-door in their neighborhoods on behalf of the slaves. These women all believed that the cause of abolition was important enough to require such unconventional activities. They were denounced, however, by men and women within the antislavery movement and without as "unfeminine" and "immoral." Such activities were believed to be beyond woman's divinely ordained sphere. The speaking activities of the Grimké sisters, for example, were strongly condemned in a widely circulated letter written by a group of Congregational clergymen, while Mott and Stanton were compelled to view the London convention from separate seating in an area screened off from the main floor.

As a result of these ideas and activities, a serious, public discussion of what came to be called the "woman question" was launched. At issue was whether or not women actually had a special sphere in life with rights and duties that differed from those of men. An organized movement for women's rights was also launched in Seneca Falls, New York, in 1848 under the leadership of Lucretia Mott and Elizabeth Cady Stanton. The women involved in this effort at first directed their attention to a broad range of concerns such as jobs, the legal rights of married women, and educational opportunities. As the century progressed, the focus shifted to the issue of women's suffrage.

Most women involved in religious, reform, and benevolent groups did not move from these activities into what we today identify as feminism. Most women continued to accept the Victorian ideal of the true woman and to shape their work outside of the home according to it. Those women who questioned the ideal were denounced by the churches. Many of these women moved away from the major denominations and into more liberal groups such as the Unitarians and Theosophists, although most of them began with the conviction that the essence of the gospel affirmed female equality and the desire to win the support of the clergy.[9] While they often discarded their traditional religious beliefs, however, many of them retained a strong certainty that what they were doing was both morally right and in keeping with the will of God.

WOMEN IN MISSION

Missions were the domain of men in America from the earliest attempts of the Puritans to convert the Native Americans of Massachusetts until the early years of the nineteenth century. The missionary societies which screened candidates, raised funds, published promotional material, and supervised field work were organized and run by men. Women could participate only so far as they were willing to pray privately for the work and accompany their husbands to the annual special sermons preached to raise money for various groups. The Second Great Awakening, however, changed all this. Existing mission work was fused with a new energy and women began to take a more active role in the cause of spreading Christianity. Also, the men's societies developed into structured denominational and interdenominational groups such as the American Board of Commissioners for Foreign Missions (1810) and the Methodist Missionary Society (1819).

Origins of Women's Missionary Organizations

The Boston Female Society for Missionary Purposes, started in 1800 by Mary Webb and fourteen Baptist and Congregationalist friends, marked the beginning of a network of local women's missionary groups. Their primary activities were prayer and fund raising for the cause of missions. Many of them were "cent societies" which met weekly to collect a penny from each member while others collected fixed annual dues. Also, many were auxiliaries of the established male societies which received and disbursed the contributions to purchase catechisms, Bibles, and other religious literature. Initial interest was in mission work among the Native Americans but gradually the focus of the women shifted to overseas missions, particularly in India and China. The fact that women were meeting together outside of the home, even for missionary purposes, initially attracted some criticism. Ministers who encouraged this activity took great pains to assure the public that these women were not speaking to mixed groups nor were they taking any part in the government of the churches. By the 1820s, consequently, the female missionary society had an accepted place in American church life. The women, however, were carefully excluded from participating in the decision making of the main societies and sometimes were not even permitted to speak in their own meetings.

Work in the Mission Field

If a woman in the early nineteenth century felt called to devote her life to "spreading the light where there was darkness," her only option was to marry a missionary and go overseas as his wife. Her primary task in this mission was to emulate the Victorian ideal woman by offering her husband a serene, well-run, and comfortable home. In addition, she functioned as a teacher of morality and religion for her children and an example of Christian womanhood for the native population around her. She was expected to learn the language and take part in the work only after her household duties had been completed. The missionary wife was given no official status by the mission boards and societies, and she had no vote in running the everyday affairs of the mission station. The *Encyclopedia of Missions*, published at the end of the last century, mentions only the three wives of Adoniram Judson and contains scattered references to men who had to return home or do such and such a thing because of the health of their wives. Yet for the women in the American churches, the missionary wives made up an elite group of heroines. Women from all over the country wrote to the wives, prayed for them, and raised funds for their special projects. Admiration for the missionary wives, in fact, may have sustained the interest of women at home in world missions despite the fact that they were excluded from power and participation on the denominational boards.[10]

The male mission boards soon realized that evangelistic work in many cultures would be successful only when the women in those cultures were reached with the Christian message. Often it was the women who were most strongly devoted to non-Christian religions and often they controlled the rituals conducted within the household. Also, in keeping with popular Western views on women, the mission organizers believed that once women in a given culture had accepted the gospel, they would be powerful influences in reaching their husbands and sons. Yet in many countries, women could only be spoken to or approached by other women. In some, women were even physically separated from men, as in the zenanas (the section of the house where women were secluded) of India. Missionary wives could do little to alleviate this problem. They were burdened with the tasks of managing home and family in an often hostile environment. Also, they had little time to learn a new language. The mission societies and boards had to look elsewhere for a solution and they found it in the single women who were willing to go to the mission field.

The mission boards reluctantly began to send single women overseas in the 1820s. The American Board of Commissioners for Foreign Missions reported that the former black slave, Betsy Stockton, was sent to Hawaii in 1823, where she ran a school. She was attached there to the family of the Rev. Charles Stewart and returned to America with them two years later. In 1827, Cynthia Farrar was sent by the American Board to India as an "assistant missionary" in order to organize schools. By 1860, the American Board had appointed 138 single women to mission work but only thirty of these went overseas. The rest remained in domestic mission work in the United States, since the Board mistakenly believed that home missions offered safer and better working conditions. The appointments, however, were sporadic and made with hesitation. The mission boards generally feared criticism and even they were uncertain as to whether or not women could carry out their tasks without the strong guidance and protection of a husband. There was also tension in the field when single women joined the work. Missionary wives suspected them of being "husband hunters" and the missionaries themselves were reluctant to give the women authority or responsibility.

Women Form Their Own Mission Boards

Women in the female missionary societies had been bombarded with the message that they should give time and money to alleviate the spiritual condition and social degradation of their sisters in more backward cultures. Ministers and laymen alike stressed the "elevation of your own sex through the medium of your own sex" to many receptive American women.[11] Women, however, began to realize that missions to women and children were receiving only halfhearted attention from the mission boards. Furthermore, women were not given any representation on these boards so that they could influence policy-making decisions. In the early 1860s, therefore, women began to take the initiative and form their own boards. The first was the interdenominational Women's Union Missionary Society in 1861, followed by a board formed by Congregational women. By 1900, there were over forty such bodies in the United States. Some of the boards were totally independent, with complete control over money and policy. Others were independent but worked in close cooperation with the men. Still others were subsidiaries of the original male boards. Throughout the history of the women's boards, some men continued to hamper and oppose the new bodies. They had a deep-rooted fear that the boards represented the movement for women's rights and suffrage in disguise.

The women's boards made women a major force in world mission. Their supporters collected large sums of money for missions, a remarkable accomplishment since women found money for their own organizations over and above the family's normal church contributions. They built and ran complex national organizations. They introduced creative methods for educating church members about missions and they conducted effective publicity campaigns.

Perhaps most significantly, the women's boards elevated the status of women in the mission field. They won full "missionary" status for the missionary wives as well as an equal vote in the everyday affairs of the mission. They also made mission work overseas an option for large numbers of single women. By the early part of the twentieth century, women represented two-thirds of the church's mission force. These women taught, managed schools, published literature, orchestrated evangelization campaigns, and engaged in preaching as well. They became involved in activities not open to them in the American churches. Murilla Ingalls, for example, carried on her husband's work in China after his death. While she avoided addressing large mixed audiences and liturgical functions, she trained men in theology, biblical studies, and preaching. The home of Presbyterian Isabella Nassau was referred to as the "theological seminary" of one West African mission. She taught young men theology, church history, and "much else" to prepare them for the ministry.

Missions also provided an opportunity for women with professional medical training to use their skills. The women's boards consciously recruited female doctors to care for the health needs of non-Christian women who, in many places, could only be treated by another woman. Their services often extended beyond treatment to the teaching of medicine as well. In their religious and medical activities women not only acquired new roles but also feelings of worth and self-confidence: "The doctor who treated two hundred patients a day . . . and the itinerant preacher who spoke until midnight and was off in her jinrikisha at dawn, felt herself necessary and important."[12]

Opportunities to work in the mission field may have diverted the attention of some women from the cause of women's rights in America by giving them opportunities for freedom and professional growth overseas.[13] Certainly very few of the women involved in the missionary movement were sympathetic with radical feminism, although many did support women's suffrage. Sometimes, however, the goals of both groups coincided. Beverly Harrison reminds us that we should not underestimate the influence that the female benevolence and mission groups had in changing the ethos of the churches.[14] Some male leaders, such as the Presbyterian Robert E. Speer, changed their minds on the status of women and openly called for equality after working with the women who skillfully coordinated the mission work. The mission boards enabled women to engage in work that was useful and important. They expanded the professional opportunities for women and even prompted some women to seek formal church recognition for the ministerial tasks they were already performing. Finally, through mission work, women began to understand other cultures and became more critical of their own, including the way in which women were treated.

The cult of true womanhood gave women an opportunity to enlarge their sphere of activity and influence by sanctioning their reform, benevolence, and mission efforts. These associations nourished the spirit of feminism and from them a few women moved into the campaign for women's rights in the United States. These women were concerned with a variety of issues including the misuse of the Bible to support patriarchy and the exclusion of women from ordained and leadership offices within the churches. Chapter 7 focuses on these issues by examining the debate over female preaching and *The Woman's Bible*.

CHAPTER 7

NINETEENTH-CENTURY PREACHERS AND SCHOLARS

WOMEN IN THE EVANGELICAL TRADITION

From 1790 until the middle of the nineteenth century, the United States experienced another wave of revivals. These revivals rapidly built up the Methodist and Baptist churches and gave an evangelical character to large segments of American Protestantism. According to many estimates, about two-thirds of the new converts were women under the age of thirty.

Why were women so prominent as revival converts during this period? They may have been responding to their constant bombardment with the message that women are by nature more religious than men and have special religious duties. Also, women may have felt less and less in control of their lives as they became economically unproductive and as they could no longer depend on parents to arrange a marriage. They turned to God therefore as one who would control their destinies and fortunes. Or, by making a commitment to God, women may have been preparing themselves for marriage, which also required submission and the abandonment of frivolous youth.[1]

We normally associate evangelical groups today with the subordination and silence of women. Historians Lucille Sider Dayton and Donald Dayton make an important point, however, in reminding us that there are significant exceptions to this pattern among American evangelicals in the last century.[2] In addition to the Unitarians, Quakers, and groups discussed in chapter 8, certain evangelical groups gave a significant public role to women.

How did nineteenth-century evangelicals respond to the question of political and social rights for women? Charles Finney never explicitly included them in his list of necessary reforms. Many evangelicals, even some who supported the preaching of women, were reluctant to press for social and political equality. Some, however, displayed attitudes that had feminist tendencies. Frances Willard felt compelled to lecture on suffrage as well as temperance although she believed women needed the vote to protect the home. Some male evangelical leaders welcomed women into educational institutions and even politics. The female editor of the main Holiness magazine, *Guide To Holiness*, believed that Pentecost put an end to the inequality of women and she urged them to get involved in the labor force. Although in some quarters gains in the church were accompanied by denials of the political and social aspirations of women, the issues were bound to be raised more urgently as some women moved into roles that for centuries had been held by men.

An Expansion of Roles in the Second Great Awakening

Revival preachers called upon all Christians to spread the gospel in response to their conversions. One of the chief ways of doing this for women, of course, was in the role of mother. Religious literature is filled with stories of women who act as powerful agents of salvation for their sons and daughters. Another private means of promoting the revival of religion was letter writing. As Anne Dutton had done in the eighteenth century, women took up their pens to convert their friends and encourage new Christians.

Women, however, promoted revivals in another more public way. They frequently held prayer meetings which petitioned God for the blessing of conversions. They also counseled women who were moved to repentance by the revival preachers. Like reform and benevolent groups, the prayer meetings were encouraged by evangelical clergymen as long as the women behaved "decorously."

The evangelist Charles Finney made a notable contribution to widening the role of women in the promotion of revivals. Finney introduced a variety of new techniques to stimulate conversions in his sweep through the northeastern states. One of these "new measures" was to allow women to speak and pray before "promiscuous" (i.e., variegated) groups composed of men and women. Finney and his assistants believed that women should not be prevented from speaking about their faith if they felt deeply moved to do so. Finney's policy aroused hostility among his colleagues but he continued it. He later became a professor and then president of Oberlin College, the first college in the United States to admit women. Among Oberlin's early graduates were several leaders of the women's rights movement and Antoinette Brown, the first woman to be ordained to the ministry in the Congregational Church.

Finney and his circle, however, were not the only leaders of evangelical Christianity to endorse the public speaking of women. Luther Lee, the founder of the Wesleyan Methodist Church, reflected the thinking of John Wesley in his belief that women had a right to preach the gospel. He preached the sermon at the ordination of Antoinette Brown, pointing to female prophets in the Old Testament and women "ministers" in the New. Later in the century, the Methodist evangelist W. B. Godbey could write, "It is a God-given, blood-bought privilege, and bounden duty of the women as well as the men, to preach the gospel."[3] The large Methodist Episcopal Church issued local preaching licenses to women until 1880.

The Holiness Movement

Women were most active in the Holiness movement, which emerged within evangelical circles as the nineteenth century progressed. The Holiness movement claimed that God's grace was available not only for salvation but also was given, in a second dramatic experience, to "sanctify" or "perfect" a Christian's life. Holiness Christians believed that God gave them the power to overcome all intentional sin. Phoebe Palmer was a major force behind the movement. She traveled as an evangelist throughout the United States, Great Britain, and Canada, and it was under her influence that Catherine Booth and Frances Willard were called to public ministries. Booth did as much as her husband, William, to establish the Salvation Army. She was an outstanding revival preacher who believed firmly in the equality of women with men in all spheres. Her own marriage as well as her work in the Salvation Army were based on this principle. Frances Willard worked for a while as an assistant to Dwight Moody, speaking on women's suffrage and temperance. She served as the president of the World's Women's Christian Temperance Union for a number of years. Both Willard and Booth published written defenses of the preaching of women, using both the Bible and examples of successful female preachers in the past to make their point. In *Female Ministry*, Booth argued in the following terms: "If she have the necessary gifts, and feels herself called by the Spirit to preach, there is not a single word in the whole book of God to restrain her, but many, very many, to urge and encourage her. God says she SHALL do so, and Paul prescribed the manner in which she shall do it, and Phoebe, Junia, Philip's four daughters, and many other women, actually did preach and speak in the primitive churches."[4] Frances Willard also discussed the use of "sexist language" in the churches, complaining that preachers never referred to the women in the audience but instead spoke constantly of "men" and "brethren."

Another prominent Holiness preacher was Amanda Berry Smith, a black woman who spent the earlier part of her life as a house servant and washerwoman. She came into the Holiness movement partly under the influence of Phoebe Palmer. Despite opposition on the grounds of her race and sex, Amanda Smith began an active preaching ministry which extended to England and eventually to India and West Africa.

The Holiness movement was at first nurtured within the mainline Protestant churches, particularly the Methodist church. Gradually, however, separate Holiness denominations emerged. Women participated widely in the groups and a high percentage of Holiness ministers were women well into the twentieth century. The Church of the Nazarene guaranteed women the right to preach in its constitution of 1894. The founder of the Pilgrim Holiness Church, Seth Rees, claimed that "no Church that is acquainted with the Holy Ghost will object to the public ministry of women."[5] The Pentecostal movement which grew out of the Holiness groups continued this view on the preaching of women. Evidence of this is the celebrated ministry of the twentieth-century figure Aimee Semple McPherson, minister of the Foursquare Gospel Church.

THE DEBATE OVER WOMEN PREACHING

The opportunity for preaching that some evangelical groups gave to women raised the issue of the proper role of women in the church for all Protestants. The question became even more insistent as women moved into other professions and expanded their public activities of reform and charity. By the end of the century, most denominations had debated whether or not to sanction the preaching and teaching of women. While these discussions took place among different groups at different times, it is possible to isolate the major arguments on both sides of the issue.[6]

Those in favor of allowing women to preach made three important points. First, churches could not prohibit what women felt called by the Holy Spirit to do. The supporters of preaching women regarded this as the most persuasive argument, especially in light of the century's emphasis on the work of the Holy Spirit in the world. The black preacher Jarena Lee was able to overcome rejection because of a "holy energy" which burned in her life like a fire, permitting her to step beyond the lines convention had established. Women who did not obey the directions of the Spirit, out of a fear of men, were said to be troubled in their souls and even subject to "fits and seizures." So far as Quaker women and their Societies were concerned, they were simply instruments of God's will when exercising a preaching ministry.

The second argument was a practical one. Women were needed in new roles to extend the work of the church. Immigration, urban expansion, and the growth of science all presented challenges to American Christians. Many people felt that the churches could not afford to overlook the skills and energies of women, especially since they had a proven record as "movers and shakers" in existing efforts to spread the gospel and reform society.

Third, the Bible featured prominently in the defense of preaching women since the opposing side also based its important arguments on Scripture. Many writers claimed that the New Testament words commanding women to keep silent were written for a particular time and place and were not meant to apply to all circumstances. Instead, Gal. 3:28 was meant to be the guidepost for all Christians when it came to the status of women. Other writers spent time studying the details of Paul's words, claiming that he only prohibited married women from speaking or that he condemned the babbling and not the praying and preaching of women. Still others anticipated modern scholarship by pointing to the active preaching ministries of women such as Deborah, the Samaritan woman, and those who "labored" with Paul. Finally, the events at Pentecost, when the Holy Spirit was poured out upon the sons and daughters of the church who then prophesied, were an important guide for the Holiness groups. To many of these Christians, God was again pouring out the Holy Spirit in America, making the preaching of women appropriate.

The arguments against the preaching of women were based first and foremost on biblical material. New Testament teaching on this issue, it was said, was clear and grounded in reasons that were not affected by the passage of time: Woman was created after man and as his helper, and woman brought sin into the world. One writer claimed that "she made a little speech once and that was the world's undoing: now let her keep silence."[7] Furthermore, since the Holy Spirit dictated the Scriptures, that same Spirit could not be self-contradictory and call a woman to preach.

Christians who objected to this wider role for women also argued on the basis of Victorian ideas of true womanhood. Some claimed, for example, that women already played an important role in the churches in their own "sphere" as mothers and as members of female religious groups. Women could be given willingly an active, speaking role in small prayer meetings and in small sex-segregated social gatherings; these meetings, however, were quite different from large "promiscuous" assemblies.

Finally, a host of social and historical reasons were used to attack those who allowed women to preach. A pregnant woman and nursing mother, for example, could not bear the exhausting duty of preaching. Also, how could a woman combine household duties and the demands on a preacher (and the church certainly did not want to discourage marriage)? Then there was the question of proper education in many denominations. Women simply did not have minds suited to theological studies. They were intuitive rather than logical and reasonable, and their preaching therefore would not win back the men so desperately needed by American congregations.

Ordination to the Ministry of
Word and Sacrament

The question of whether or not churches should ordain women to a ministry was also an issue in the nineteenth century. In most Christian traditions, ordination is understood as the setting apart of certain individuals to hold special authority within the congregation, usually authority to preach, administer the sacraments, and supervise the affairs of the congregation. Because of the central role that preaching played in the tasks of the ordained clergy in most Christian groups, the issue of ordination was very closely related to that of preaching.

Although they had no sacramental ministry, the Unitarians and Universalists ordained women in the nineteenth century. Some Congregationalist churches also made the decision, on the local level, to ordain women. The first was Antoinette Brown who, in 1853, was ordained to a charge in East Butler, New York. By 1900, there were forty ordained women in Congregationalist churches. Baptist congregations could in theory have decided to ordain women but it is not clear whether they did so in practice. Although the Methodist Episcopal Church rejected the requests in 1880 of Anna Howard Shaw and Anna Oliver, the Methodist Protestant Church, a small branch of the Methodist family, ordained Shaw a short time later. Another branch of the Methodist family, the Wesleyan Methodists, had agreed to ordain women in the 1860s. Despite the fact that the issue was raised in a number of other denominations, groups such as the Lutherans, Presbyterians, and Episcopalians did not admit women to the ordained ministry until well into the twentieth century (with the exception of the Cumberland Presbyterian Church, which began to ordain women in 1889).

Generally, women who hoped to be ordained to the ministry in the last century faced a lonely struggle, even within sympathetic denominations. A Woman's Ministerial Conference was formed in 1882 to provide a network of support for women but it had little power to enact changes. Some theological schools such as those at Oberlin and Boston University admitted women, but aspiring candidates faced strenuous opposition at local and national levels of church life.

The Deaconess Movement

In many Protestant denominations, professional church work was initially opened to women through the office of deaconess. Nineteenth-

century Christians believed that they were restoring a New Testament office. They interpreted the early office, however, as one of service to the
community without any liturgical functions or formal ordination. It is important therefore to distinguish between these "deaconesses" and the "female deacons" who would come to have equal duties with the male deacons in the twentieth century.

The movement in the United States was inspired by the deaconess community in Kaiserswerth, Germany, founded by Theodore Fliedner in
1836. It first appeared in America in 1849 but was not widespread until
after the Civil War when the Lutheran, Episcopalian, Methodist, and Presbyterian churches made provisions for the position. Women who volun-
teered to be deaconesses were set apart by prayer and special training for
work as nurses, social workers, and missionaries. They were particularly
influential as social workers in immigrant communities in which they ran
schools, hospitals, and settlement houses.

For a variety of reasons, the office of deaconess was never very attractive
to women in the United States.[8] It is possible that many women found
enough channels for activity and leadership in the societies for reform
and mission. Also, anti-Catholic sentiment shed suspicion on groups of
women who dressed in plain, dark uniforms or who, as the Lutheran deaconesses did, lived in motherhouses under strict regulations. They reminded the Protestant public of "popish" convents and religious orders.
There was also the fear that the office of deaconess would be seen as a step-
pingstone to ordination for women. Those who supported the deaconesses had to emphasize that women were not ordained to the office and
that they were working within their designated "sphere" by simply ex-
tending their responsibilities as mothers and household managers.

THE WOMAN'S BIBLE

When nineteenth-century women tried to get the vote, access to the
professions, and a wider role in the churches, they were met with the argument that these activities were not only "unnatural" but they were also
against the commands of the Bible. One of the resolutions drawn up at the
Seneca Falls Convention denounced the "perverted application of the
Scriptures" which restricted and degraded women. It was not until the
1880s, however, that women took up the task of systematically exploring
the actual status of women in the Bible. The result was *The Woman's Bible*,
published in two parts in 1895 and 1898.

The publication is not an attempt to purge the Bible of its masculine-
oriented language or of the parts that women found degrading. Rather,

The Woman's Bible is a series of commentaries or observations prepared by a committee of women on those parts of the Bible that deal with women. The writers tried to argue for women's rights on the same grounds that their opponents used to argue against them—the Scriptures of the Old and New Testaments. *The Woman's Bible* is therefore an attempt to reclaim the Bible for feminism. Its writers believed that by doing so, a major obstacle would be removed from the path of equality for women.

Elizabeth Cady Stanton was the chief architect of the publication. Her life reflected the experiences shared by most of the women on the committee. They tended to be well-educated, disillusioned with traditional Protestant Christianity, and concerned with acquiring a broad range of rights for women and not simply the vote. Stanton grew up in a Presbyterian family in Johnstown, Pennsylvania. She associated the Christian faith with cold churches and gloomy sermons, but she remained grateful to the family's pastor, who thought enough of her ability to teach her Greek. Cady Stanton, however, was also profoundly affected by a young man who had been helped through seminary by the girls' club to which she belonged. After they had provided for his education and given him a new suit upon his graduation, he preached his first sermon on the text, "But I suffer not a woman to teach . . . but to be in silence" (1 Tim. 2:12).

Her concern for the rights of women was shaped by several influences. Listening to the clients of her father, an attorney and judge, Cady Stanton had become aware of the severe legal disabilities of married women. Her own frustration as a mother and housekeeper moved her to rebel against the doctrine of "woman's sphere." Also, her experiences in the antislavery campaign made her keenly aware of the obstacles and prejudice women faced. She devoted her life to the cause of women's rights, advocating a wide spectrum of rights for women in the church, the workplace, and the home. She eventually became convinced that little could be done until women collectively recognized their subjection and rejected it. Yet this could not happen until the spell that the Bible had cast upon them was broken. She therefore set about the task of seeing whether or not the Bible was "usable" in the quest for women's rights.

The commentaries written by the women Cady Stanton gathered around her were strongly influenced by the movements and events of their world. They reflect the current belief that the Bible was not an infallible letter from God to the human race but was a human book which was written in a number of cultural contexts. They did not deny, however, that the Bible contained divine truth.

The writers viewed God as a benevolent Creator who had established laws for the smooth operation of the world. These laws demanded justice and equal access to liberty and happiness for all human beings. The universe was so ordered that a balance between the feminine and the masculine had to be acknowledged in everyday life. In God, the women believed that they had an ally for their cause. The Bible had to be brought under the judgment of these divinely ordained laws just like all other human enterprises. Where women were found to be treated with justice and humanity in the Bible, it was possible to speak of such material as the "Word of God." Where women were degraded and made subordinate, the Bible could be given no such status. This kind of material merely reflected the male domination of the cultures in which it developed.

With these theological ideas in mind, the women took upon themselves the task of preparing commentaries on passages which had been assigned to each of them. The commentaries do several things. They bring to attention and celebrate women who asserted their rights and dignity. They reinterpret some parts in which the message of female equality has been hidden or overlooked. They also expose those sections that they found to devalue women and they question the divine origins of such passages.

Much of their work is remarkably similar to biblical scholarship being conducted by women today. Stanton's committee was eager to uncover false teachings that distorted the gospel. In commenting on Num. 20: 1–16, for example, Rev. Phoebe Hanaford denounced the fact that a woman could not be responsible for her vow to God. She claimed that this passage portrays women as irresponsible children rather than as mature adults with the freedom intended by God: "It is unjust to a man that he should have the added responsibility of his daughter's or wife's word, and it is cruel to a woman because the irresponsibility is enslaving in its influence. It is contrary to true Gospel teaching, for only in freedom to do right can a soul dwell in that love which is the fulfilling of the law."[9] In the discussion of 1 Corinthians 11, the commentator informs her readers that God did not command women to cover their heads. Rather, the command originated in an ancient Hebrew myth about the sons of God and the daughters of men.

The women, however, were just as eager to present the biblical message of liberation. Vashti is applauded by *The Woman's Bible* as a woman who threw off the tyranny of her husband and refused to be treated simply as a sex object. The daughters of Zelophehad, who stood up to Moses and argued for their inheritance, are rescued from oblivion. Deborah and Huldah are designated as role models for nineteenth-century women and Jesus' treatment of women as fully human and worthy of respect is emphasized.

It was in reinterpreting or reformulating tradition, however, that Stanton and her committee did their most formidable work. Two examples can give us some idea of this process. Using the insights of biblical scholars, the women distinguished between the two accounts of creation in Genesis 1 and Genesis 2—3. Genesis 1 was treated as divine truth because it reflected the great divine laws of masculine and feminine equality which were built into God's creation: "If language has any meaning, we have in these texts a plain declaration of the existence of the feminine element in the Godhead, equal in power and glory with the masculine."[10] Genesis 2—3, however, showed the perverse influence of male-dominated culture over the biblical author. The creation of the woman is described in a demeaning way and woman is made the scapegoat for the man's sin.

The New Testament parable of the wise and foolish virgins (Matt. 25:1 –12) was also given a significant new interpretation. Jesus, the women claimed, used the story to encourage the self-reliance of women. The wise virgins in their commentary are compared to women who have cultivated their own skills and talents. The foolish virgins are like those women who totally sacrifice themselves to the success of men while burying their own capacities and powers. The latter group will be unprepared to meet the personal crises of life as well as the demands of modern society.

At the time of its publication, *The Woman's Bible* was greeted with hostility and ridicule. Even the National American Woman Suffrage Association passed a resolution denying any association with the *Bible*. To tamper with the Scriptures was to invite the anger of evangelical women on whom the group had come to depend for support. Yet Cady Stanton and her committee, while not equipped with the same critical tools, anticipated twentieth-century feminist theology and biblical scholarship by reinterpreting the tradition, recognizing the patriarchal context of the biblical writers, and identifying lost traditions affirming women.

As in colonial America, some segments of the evangelical community in the nineteenth century encouraged women to preach and speak in public. For most American Christians, however, the case against female preaching was stated plainly in the Bible along with the doctrine of separate spheres and female subordination. Yet was this material to be understood as the revealed Word of God? The editors of *The Woman's Bible* answered No and instead claimed that divine revelation affirmed the equality and full humanity of women. The debates over preaching and biblical interpretation occurred mainly among American Protestants from the major denominations. There were other significant developments for the status of women in Christianity in the last century, but for these we must look to the Catholic community and to a variety of sectarian groups.

CHAPTER 8

AMERICAN WOMEN IN CATHOLICISM AND SECTARIANISM

IMAGES OF WOMEN IN AMERICAN CATHOLICISM

Roman Catholics were viewed with suspicion in most of the American colonies in the seventeenth and eighteenth centuries. Opportunities for free worship were restricted and Catholic believers made up only a very small percentage of the American population. American Catholic and French Catholic support for the American Revolution, plus the new republic's promise of freedom of religion, created a new social climate for the Catholic Church at the beginning of the nineteenth century. The century became one of rapid expansion and major challenges. The church developed a hierarchy of bishops and archbishops, opened schools, and published newspapers. Also, its membership grew dramatically as a result of waves of immigrants coming from Europe. At the same time, Catholicism faced continued hostility from some American Protestants, a need to keep the faith alive on the frontier and in the swelling cities, and a new culture which sometimes clashed with a religion shaped in medieval Europe.

The role of women in American Catholic history has been largely ignored by historians who survey either American religion in general or Catholicism in particular. There are references to several outstanding women who established religious orders in America. One modern textbook mentions women once and only in the chapter on "Social Hysteria." Some historians such as Mary Ewens, however, have begun to explore Catholic women in religious orders as a group, asking questions about their self-perception, their work, and their relationship to women outside the convent walls.[1] Others, such as James Keneally, have explored the church's official attitudes toward women and women's issues and raise the question of whether women really shaped their lives accordingly.[2]

The Cult of True Womanhood
in Catholic Thought

The cult of true womanhood was reflected as much in Catholic views of women as in those of white American Protestants. It was a familiar and acceptable cluster of ideas for Catholic Americans and has continued to be endorsed by the church through much of the twentieth century. Both church tradition and the Bible, most Catholics believed, taught that women were to be submissive and domestic. The figure of the Virgin Mary confirmed these characteristics and reinforced the Victorian ideal of women as morally pure, sexless creatures who bring redemption to the sinful world. Catholic women were called upon to be submissive wives and mothers who could be "regal" and "heroic" in their own sphere but who would endanger civilization and thwart the purposes of God by seeking jobs or the vote or equality with men.

The Catholic adoption of Victorian true womanhood provided the framework in which the movement for women's suffrage was regarded. Many of the clergy believed that suffrage would undermine the family and civilization. The bishop of Colorado, Joseph Macheboeuf, dismissed the suffragists as "old maids" who had been disappointed in love. Other Catholic leaders regarded suffrage as an "unspiritual abnormality" which would tear woman from her pedestal and leave her stained and bleeding in the dirty world of politics. The National American Woman Suffrage Association in 1900 could only count on the support of six Catholic clergymen. There is also some evidence that the message of the clergy was taken seriously by lay men and women. Only one officer of the women's suffrage association was Catholic and very few became involved in organized feminism generally. Studies have been conducted showing that in the Massachusetts referendum on suffrage in 1895, the Catholic sections of the state were overwhelmingly against the right of women to vote.

While not deviating from popular Victorian views on the special nature and function of women, a few Catholic leaders defended suffrage. Bishop John Spaulding in 1884, for example, believed that pious and pure women could use their votes to elevate American society. The Catholic women's suffrage groups, which sprang up late in the movement, believed that women could use their political power to halt the radical feminist attempts to ruin the family by taking women beyond their divinely ordained sphere.

Catholic ideas on the education of women also reflected the popular ideal of true womanhood. Mary, the mother of Jesus, was the role model women were encouraged to imitate. She was wife and mother and had no need for academic training. Consequently, many Catholic leaders claimed that the knowledge that came from newspapers and books was unbecoming to a woman. This argument was modified by a significant number of lay and clerical voices urging that women be given "special education" in order to make them better wives and mothers. A curriculum tailored to woman's role and nature was approved for the institutions of higher education that began to appear. Any advanced schooling given to women was to concentrate on teaching them modesty along with domestic and child-rearing skills.

Not only was a voting and educated woman a danger to society, so also was a woman who was employed outside the home. Such an arrangement violated the divine order which dictated that a woman give herself totally to the well-being of her husband and children. Employment also put women in positions in which their virtue could be compromised. Yet many Catholic women, particularly immigrants of the late nineteenth century, were forced to seek employment away from home out of economic necessity. Some Catholic leaders urged therefore that men should be paid higher wages on which a family could exist, thus making it unnecessary for women to work. The social activist John Ryan campaigned for a minimum wage for workers which would stop employers from hiring women as cheap sources of labor. Other Catholics such as Leonora Barry urged women to join the Knights of Labor in order to advocate working conditions befitting the purity and sensitivity of women. While very few Catholic leaders approved of women working outside of the home, many conceded that since some women were forced to earn a living, employers should be encouraged to make every effort to protect true womanhood.

Eve Lingers On

Although Protestants had not entirely forgotten the image of Eve as the archetypal woman who sins and seduces, American Catholics placed more emphasis on woman as temptress. Women might be the guardians of virtue and morality, but they could just as easily be the perpetuators of sin. Following the example of the church fathers, American bishops warned women against immodest dress and the use of cosmetics. An early twentieth-century article in a Catholic encyclopedia reverted to the tradition of earlier centuries in claiming woman's moral and spiritual inferiority. Girls and boys were segregated in Catholic schools to prevent the "corruption" of young men. Catholic colleges were also strictly segregated until financial necessity prompted some men's schools to become coeducational. A book on pastoral care at the end of the nineteenth century warned priests not to fall victim to the snares of "American Eves" who came to confess their sins.

AMERICAN WOMEN IN RELIGIOUS ORDERS

Women as members of religious orders first came to the United States in the early seventeenth century as a part of European efforts to colonize and Christianize North America. Their membership grew to over forty thousand by 1900 and in the 1970s an official Catholic directory listed 450 women's orders in the United States. It is only recently that their contribution to American Catholicism and society as a whole has been examined by historians. It is also only recently that the significance of convent life for American Catholic women in the last century has been explored.

As early as the 1630s, women who belonged to religious orders in the French territories of Quebec and Montreal worked as missionaries to the Native Americans and became involved in a wide variety of educational and nursing enterprises. Spanish American sisters also made significant contributions to the education of young women in the New World. The convents and the virgin life continued to function for these women much as they did in the early centuries of Christian history—as places of economic security, female autonomy, self-expression, and the nurturing of faith. Juana Ines de la Cruz, for example, found an outlet for her intellectual and literary skills in a Mexican convent where she produced plays, poetry, and theological works. Such women often endured harsh climates, destructive fires, and hostile European and native neighbors in order to establish their vision of the Christian life in the new territories.

The scope of the projects undertaken by Catholic sisters in the nineteenth century demonstrates that they were largely unaffected by the Victorian advice that frail woman should be passive and protected. The sisters throughout America founded and ran a multitude of social services in an era when new frontier settlements and rapidly growing cities had no organized social services. The sisters provided homes for unwed mothers and delinquent girls. They cared for the aged and mentally ill and opened day-care centers. Their services in teaching school and in nursing the sick, however, became hallmarks of Catholic concern for others as well as vehicles for better relationships between Protestant and Catholic Americans.

The Catholic Church was faced with a variety of challenges in the nineteenth century and the women in religious orders did a great deal to aid the church in meeting them successfully. On two specific fronts, there is evidence that the women accomplished considerably more than the male hierarchy of priests and bishops.

Educational Endeavors

One important challenge to the church was the preservation of the Catholic faith among dislocated families on the frontier or in urban ethnic ghettos. Children particularly had to be reached and taught basic Catholic beliefs, a task increasingly being neglected by parents. The women of the Catholic orders responded to this desperate need by making teaching one of their chief occupations in America. By 1900 they ran and staffed most of the nearly four thousand parochial schools in the country as well as over six hundred girls' academies. In addition to basic educational skills, the sisters taught religion and Christian living to the children. Many of the schools were established and run by sisters from Europe who possessed a knowledge of some of the best educational theory available.

In addition to seeing that Catholic Christianity was taught to children, the church also had to gain popular acceptance in a country that was largely Protestant and hostile to Catholicism. Outbreaks of anti-Catholic sentiment occurred throughout the century, fired by the sermons and speeches of Protestant leaders who feared that the Catholic faith was a danger to true religion and democracy. The Catholic sisters and their convents were often targets of this hostility. Because of their distinctive dress, they were easy to spot on the street and frequently, like Mother Caroline Friess, pelted with mud and insulted. American Protestants were threatened by the aura of mystery that surrounded the convent with its European customs and "undemocratic," authoritarian structure. The popular press churned out a flood of literature attacking convent life, claiming that rape and infanticide went on behind locked doors. Alleged "ex-nuns" were paraded around the country with "true confessions" about the convents. In Baltimore and St. Louis, mobs attacked convent property. Friess describes in her writings the special robes in which the sisters slept in case they had to escape from their building in the middle of the night.

The teaching services of the sisters did much to rid the American public of anti-Catholic feelings. Protestant as well as Catholic children attended the schools, especially in frontier areas, and formed bonds of respect and affection with their instructors. Parents admired the advanced methods of some of the sisters as well as their dedication to their work. But the nursing services of the sisters during the century also played a major role in winning Catholic credibility.

Nursing

Women from religious orders performed important nursing services in private homes, hospitals, and almshouses. Their willingness to nurse people with contagious diseases and their perseverance in working through epidemics of cholera and yellow fever gained them the admiration of the public. During the Civil War they represented one fifth of the nurses on the battlefield and they were active in the Spanish American War as well. They not only offered healing skills to many war casualties but they also provided counseling and friendship. Sister Bridget Pleets, a member of an American Indian sisterhood, contacted the relatives of dying soldiers who had written their names and addresses on her apron. Mary Ewens, who has written extensively on the American nuns, believes that the Civil War marks a real watershed in the history of American attitudes toward Catholics. Through actual contact with the work of these women, a large segment of the population saw the Catholic faith in a more favorable light.

The Catholic sisters not only aided the church by teaching its doctrine and making it more acceptable to Americans; they also gave the church a firmer footing in America by recognizing that its structures had to adapt to new cultural conditions. The rules governing the women's communities in Europe (which were brought over to the United States) were developed during the Middle Ages when women were viewed as childlike, irresponsible, and in need of constant supervision. They were "cloistered" or shut away from the rest of the world. Their schools and churches were in adjacent buildings and visitors could, with special permission, see the sisters only in a parlor where they were separated by a grill. In America, however, the school or church might be some distance from the convent. Also, the social tasks that needed to be accomplished made cloistered life seem less appropriate. Many of the orders therefore sought to have their constitutions changed or replaced in order to respond to new demands.

As it did from the early centuries of the church, the religious order offered certain benefits to women which they could not get elsewhere. Ewens suggests that the Catholic sisters were in fact the most "liberated" women in nineteenth-century America. She observes that while the sisters did not have the political influence and wealth that some of their predecessors had in medieval times, they still enjoyed many opportunities to use their talents. They owned property, held executive positions, and were often encouraged to acquire an advanced education. They enjoyed the support of other women and frequently were treated as friends and colleagues by the bishops and priests with whom they worked. They undertook meaningful and useful work and they were urged to cultivate every personal gift "for the Creator's honor and glory." Like other women, the sisters were not admitted to the ordained offices of the church. Like their predecessors in the virgin life, the benefits they acquired were contingent upon their vow to hide their femaleness under thick layers of black cloth. They did, however, represent an attractive alternative to marriage and motherhood for American Catholic women. We are left to think about the question of whether women who had this alternative were less likely to get involved with organized feminism and the movement for women's rights.

WOMEN AND SECTARIAN CHRISTIANITY

Religious groups which historians refer to as "sects" appeared in many locations in America throughout the nineteenth century. The word "sect" is used not to degrade or ridicule these groups but to indicate that they withdrew or broke away from the religious tradition that dominated America during this period—evangelical Protestant Christianity. It is also helpful to know that the word "sect" comes from the Latin word "sequi," which means "to follow." Many of the sectarian groups were founded and led by dominant, charismatic personalities who wielded power and who were regarded as divinely inspired by God. In several groups, these leaders were women.

There are probably many reasons that sectarian groups flourished in nineteenth-century America. Certainly they were influenced by the atmosphere of revival excitement. They may have been expressions of alienation on the part of people who could not conform, for whatever reasons, to the economic and social demands of American culture. Often the sectarian groups claimed that the American churches had compromised too much with the world and Satan, and had forsaken the true faith.

While the sectarian groups were critical of mainstream Protestant Christianity, they often adopted and accentuated the beliefs of the traditional churches. Some groups, for example, emphasized the possibility that the Christian, through the blessings of the Holy Spirit, could live a perfect or "sanctified" life free from all intentional sin. Others stressed the second coming of Jesus and in some instances claimed that this had already taken place. Almost all of the groups accepted the idea that God continued to reveal new spiritual truth to believers which necessitated a reinterpretation of the Bible.

We are interested in examining the status of women in sectarian Christianity. We will also consider whether women were attracted to these groups and if so, why. There were many sectarian groups in nineteenth-century America and it is possible to refer to only a handful in exploring these questions. Five groups in particular are relevant to our discussion of women in the Christian tradition. Two of these are movements in which members lived together in communes in which all property was held in common and in which life styles and beliefs were highly regulated. The Shakers, founded by the Englishwoman Ann Lee at the end of the eighteenth century, spread their celibate and simple life style from Maine to Kentucky in the next several decades. The community in Oneida, New York, led by John Humphrey Noyes, was influenced by the prevailing belief that Christians could overcome all intentional sin. Noyes believed that

Oneida represented God's kingdom on earth where selfishness, sexual inequality, tiresome labor, and death itself would be overcome.

While the Shakers dwindled in numbers and the Oneida community disbanded, two other sectarian groups flourished into the twentieth century and acquired wealthy and powerful national organizations. The charismatic leader Ellen Gould White founded the Seventh-Day Adventists on the basis of her belief that Jesus would come again if worship was conducted on the Jewish Sabbath. Mary Baker Eddy, the architect of Christian Science and the author of *Science and Health*, launched a new sectarian group which claimed that the material world, including pain and disease, was illusory. God (and the human reflection of the divine image) was the only reality, and a person could be trained to live on that level of reality only. Finally, there were the Spiritualists who flourished in the middle of the century. Their belief was in the reality of life after death and in the ability of the living to communicate with the dead through professional mediums. Although many people were serious believers in Spiritualism, the movement did not succeed in building a national organization that lasted any length of time.

Challenges to the Victorian Ideal

Both the Shakers and the Oneida Community dramatically altered the Victorian picture of the ideal woman as wife, mother, and keeper of the hearth. The family was seen as a stumbling block to these groups since it diverted the attention and efforts of women and men away from the good of the community. Even before the Shakers were organized into communes, they had solved this potential problem by adopting a life of celibacy. Ann Lee claimed that she had received a vision from Jesus revealing to her that the original sin of Adam and Eve was sexual intercourse to satisfy their animal lusts. The perfect or sinless life therefore was a life without sexual desire or sexual relations. The Shaker community included both men and women, but celibacy was strictly enforced through indoctrination and careful regulation of day-to-day activities. Shaker hymns repeated the message that "By a pois'nous fleshy nature, this dark world has long been led. . . . "[4] Men and women ate at different tables, worked separately, used separate stairs to their living quarters, and sat on opposite sides of the room for worship.

John Humphrey Noyes had a different solution to the problem of the traditional family. He rejected celibacy and instead proposed a system of "complex marriage" in which every man in the community was married to every woman and vice versa. Noyes claimed that sexual relations were a gift from God which would not disappear in the kingdom but rather would be extended to include all the saints instead of just one husband given to one wife. This, he believed, was the meaning of the phrase, "They shall neither marry nor be given in marriage." The leaders of the community regulated the frequency of sexual liaisons between men and women, insisting that they did not condone "free love" and also making sure that no permanent attachments developed. Women, however, were encouraged to take the initiative in beginning relationships and Noyes expressed particular concern that they be sexually satisfied by their partners. To reduce the chances of pregnancy, Noyes taught a method of birth control in which the male partner could, through discipline, eliminate the ejaculation of sperm during sexual intercourse.

In addition to challenging the Victorian ideal of the family, the Shakers and residents of Oneida also challenged the idea of male and female occupational "spheres." The communities were self-sufficient, producing the products and food necessary for daily life. They were similar to the pre-industrial households of colonial America. In both instances, women had useful and productive work to fill their days. In the Shaker villages, women generally did the indoor work and men did the heavier outdoor tasks but there was no indication that one type of work was superior to the other. There is also evidence that men in Shaker communes carded wool and picked fruit, duties normally assigned to women. At Oneida, where men and women freely intermingled, women farmed alongside of men and men learned to sew. Women, it seems, were also encouraged to drive the teams of horses and work in the machine shops. Child rearing also became a shared responsibility. Orphans and the children of new converts among the Shakers were cared for by a group of adults. The Oneida Community discouraged the formation of bonds between mothers and children and relegated their care to men and women of the community in a special wing of the house.

Some of the sectarian groups not only altered basic ideas in the cult of true womanhood, but they also challenged traditional theological concepts. Both Noyes and Eddy insisted that God had masculine as well as feminine dimensions or elements. Often the word *androgynous* (having the characteristics or nature of male and female) is used to describe their perspective. Eddy emphasized that this did not mean that God had the physical characteristics of male and female, but rather that God included both the masculine attributes of Intelligence and Truth and the feminine quality of Love. In fact, to the created world God was more feminine than masculine, being known primarily through works of love. She encouraged her followers to reflect the divine image by showing both masculine and feminine characteristics.

This dual nature of God was not always reflected in the other beliefs and organizational structures of the sectarian communities. The Shakers, however, used their belief in the androgynous nature of God as a keystone in the life of the community. They built into their theology and group structures an equal role for women. Just as God the Father had come to earth in the form of Jesus, so God the Mother came in the person of Ann Lee, the Second Messiah. With the coming of the female Messiah, the original equality that woman had with man was restored. The Shaker Ministry which presided over the community was made up of two women and two men. An equal number of Elders and Eldresses supervised the spiritual life of the Shaker "families" (thirty to ninety people) while Deacons and Deaconesses attended to the practical details of communal life.

New Opportunities for Participation

Other sectarian groups offered women opportunities for participation and recognition which went beyond what was available to them in traditional Protestant churches. Although Eddy used men to fill administrative positions, she sent women throughout the country to communicate her message. Augusta Stetson was responsible for establishing the enormously prestigious First Church of Christ, Scientist in New York. Eddy also employed women as practitioners of healing within the movement. The rituals of worship in Christian Science churches were also led by a male and female reader from the congregation.

The Spiritualists also availed themselves of the services of women as well as men in their quest for contact with the spiritual world. The number of female mediums operating in the United States in 1859, for example, was 121 as compared to 110 men. The Spiritualists claimed in fact that the feminine traits of passiveness, strong feelings, and weak reason made women very suitable for such a role.

Perhaps most significantly, the sectarian groups were prepared to see women as inspired channels for new truth from God. Both Ann Lee and Eddy offered new interpretations of traditional Christian concepts which were regarded as authoritative by their followers. Ellen Gould White's visions, committed to writing with the assistance of her husband, not only shaped the beliefs of the Seventh-Day Adventists but also guided her followers in matters of health care, diet, and dress. She and Eddy exercised almost unquestioned power for decades over funds, buildings, mission enterprises, and a growing number of believers.

Why were women attracted to sectarianism? Generally, women have outnumbered men among those Americans who became involved with sectarian groups. In Christian Science, for example, roughly three women for every man joined while women outnumbered men six to one as practitioners of healing. Studies of some Shaker communities in the last century show two female members for every male on an average, although women more dramatically outnumbered men in the age bracket of twenty to forty-five years. These statistics may simply reflect what was true in the traditional churches out of which many sectarian members came. It is possible, however, to suggest that women may have been attracted to the sectarian communities for reasons directly related to their status in church and society.

Evidence taken from the direct testimonies and experiences of women helps to uncover some of their motivations.[5] Women believed that by joining groups such as the Shakers and Adventists, their search for eternal salvation would be ended. The revival spirit created an atmosphere of intense religious feelings and yearnings which were satisfied for some women in sectarianism. Also, contact with other women, especially in the communal sects, seemed to provide some women with a much-needed sense of sisterhood. Testimonies from Shaker women, for example, reveal their intense enjoyment of conversation with women in their own communities and visits and letters from sisters in other locations. Finally, for mothers, both married and widowed, life in a religious community offered the assurance that should death strike, their children would be cared for and the family unit would not be broken up. Widows and single women also found more immediate benefits in the economic security offered by the commune.

By joining the sectarian groups, however, women may also have been unconsciously rebelling against their status in the Protestant churches and in American culture.[6] This motivation is difficult to document because women were probably reluctant to express outright their distaste for childbirth or sexual intercourse or housekeeping or masculine language for God. Yet we must at least consider the possibility that they were drawn to sectarianism because they were attracted to rituals that included women, symbols that appreciated the feminine, and styles of living in which they could break the bonds of woman's traditional "sphere."

Christian Science and Spiritualism may have been particularly attractive to women who were unconsciously dissatisfied with their traditional roles. It is possible that a cluster of ailments known as "hysteria" in the nineteenth century provided women with a way to escape the duties of household management and sexual intercourse. Christian Science may have "cured" some women of their illness by offering them alternative roles as practitioners, readers, and missionaries.[7] Spiritualism, in a different kind of way, may have enabled women to deal with their discontent.[8] In a state of trance and under the control of the spirit world, women who were mediums sometimes assumed masculine roles such as swearing sailors or brilliant scholars that were denied to them in real life. They won attention and public acclaim for themselves as well, generally without the condemnation that they were going beyond their sphere since they were not responsible for what was happening.

American Catholicism and sectarianism, movements outside the Protestant mainstream, reveal familiar themes in the history of women in the Christian tradition. The cult of true womanhood was preached by the Catholic hierarchy and educational establishment, while the virgin life continued to offer some women a chance for autonomy and influence in church and society. At the same time, groups on the fringe of the dominant evangelical Protestant denominations expanded the boundaries of "woman's sphere" in radical ways. As America moved into the twentieth century, however, women within the established denominations began to seek and assume new positions of leadership and ministry.

CHAPTER 9

THE MOVE TOWARD FULL PARTICIPATION

Historians of many dimensions of human life often refer to the First World War as a watershed. Philosophy, technology, and theology in the 1920s and 1930s were markedly different from their Victorian counterparts. In a sense, the war was also a watershed for women in the Christian community. In the decade that followed, discussion of the "woman question" in the churches reached a new level of intensity, and a sustained movement advocating full participation for women in the churches was begun. Although that movement subsequently faltered and faded, it has resulted in the current growing acceptance of women in a full range of ecclesiastical duties and roles.

Events both inside and outside the Christian community gave rise to this burst of interest in the status of women. Women had shown skill and initiative in filling a variety of jobs while men served in the armed forces. Their war relief efforts, particularly in fund raising and nursing, enhanced their status in the public eye. Even before the war, the number of women in medicine, law, and teaching had begun to make small but significant increases. The Nineteenth Amendment giving women the right to vote was ratified in August of 1920, raising questions about what women would do with their new-found political power. Finally, the churches became aware of a new critical approach to the Bible which had originated in Germany. The new or "higher" criticism emphasized the historical circumstances out of which the New Testament restrictions on women grew and questioned their appropriateness for the twentieth century.

THE EXPANSION OF DENOMINATIONAL ROLES

In some denominations, women asserted their right to address publicly "mixed" or male audiences, particularly at national gatherings. Often they did so as representatives of women's missionary work. Katharine Bennett of the Women's Board of Home Missions, for example, was the first woman to bring a formal report before the General Assembly of the Presbyterian Church in the U.S.A. in 1916. Two years later, two Baptist laywomen addressed the Southern Baptist Convention on behalf of the Woman's Baptist Missionary Union Training School.

Speaking privileges at all levels of institutional life accompanied the election or appointment of women to lay offices. As early as 1904, women were included as lay participants in the conferences of the Methodist Episcopal Church. In the 1920s and 1930s delegate status was opened to women in some Lutheran Synods and in the Methodist Episcopal Church South. Helen Barrett Montgomery was elected President of the Northern Baptist Convention in 1921. Even the conference on Faith and Order in Lausanne, Switzerland, included seven women who gathered with hundreds of men to discuss the unity of the church.

Very few women sought ordination in the 1920s although there were small gains in those denominations that did open the ordained ministry to women. By 1927 there were one hundred women serving as the ordained pastors of Congregational churches and there were slightly more in the Disciples of Christ. The Cumberland Presbyterian Church continued to ordain a handful of women and the Unitarians and Universalists held to their practices established in the nineteenth century. Two larger denominations—the Methodist Episcopal Church and the Presbyterian Church in the U.S.A.—took significant steps toward full clerical rights for women.

In 1920 the Methodists again granted local preaching licenses to women, and by 1926 opened ordination as elders to them, enabling them to preach, conduct worship, administer the sacraments, and perform marriages. The women elders, however, were to restrict their activities to a local congregation. They could not participate in a traveling ministry. By 1928 there were sixteen women serving local congregations as ordained elders.

The Presbyterians in 1922 voted to ordain women as deacons in local churches. They were to exercise the same rights and fulfill the same responsibilities as the male deacons. Several years earlier, the United Presbyterian Church of North America had taken the same step. Many members of the Presbyterian Church in the U.S.A., however, believed that women should be granted representation in the church courts and should be admitted to the ordained ministry. A committee was established by the Gen eral Assembly to study the status of women, and women themselves organized several efforts to secure ordination rights. A 1929 overture giv· ing women full equality was not approved at the presbytery level, but an overture allowing them to be ordained as elders was passed. Sarah L.

Dickson, a religious educator from the Presbytery of Milwaukee, was the first woman in the denomination to be ordained as an elder.

These changes in ordination policies were accompanied by some changes in the admission policies of theological seminaries. In the late nineteenth and early twentieth centuries, very few schools admitted women to a full theological curriculum. Some notable exceptions were Boston University's School of Theology, Oberlin School of Theology, and Union Theological Seminary (New York) which graduated its first woman, Emilie Grace Briggs, in 1897. In 1920 Hartford Seminary (Congregational) admitted women without the explicit declaration that they did not intend to enter the ordained ministry.

SIGNS OF RETRENCHMENT

In the period following World War I, the positions of deaconess and missionary continued to be the only professional options for women in many denominations. There were attempts to make the position of deaconess more attractive to women by upgrading the image and educational requirements for the job. In many instances, however, the position retained the connotation of subservient and second-class "errand girl." In 1920 the Episcopal Church, guided by the Church of England, regarded the deaconess as a member of the clergy and as the recipient of Holy Orders. The decision was reversed, however, in 1930.

Women continued to be active both as the staff and the support network of home and foreign missions. They became a major force in world mission, outnumbering men in the mission field by two to one by 1929. Yet the work of women in the first quarter of the twentieth century was overshadowed by efforts to merge the mission boards controlled by women with the denominational boards controlled by men. These efforts, for example, succeeded in the Presbyterian Church in the U.S.A. in 1923 and two years later in the Congregational churches. The women's boards were eliminated at the national level and their budgets were combined with those of the male-dominated associations. At the same time the women's missionary training colleges were closed or absorbed into the theological seminaries which began to teach practical subjects such as religious education and to supervise student field work.

The main reason voiced for these changes was the efficiency that centralization would bring. The mission historian R. Pierce Beaver suggests that churchmen feared the diversion of funds away from the family's regular contributions to the church. He also suggests that the expense of the mission work directed by the male-dominated boards invited unfavorable comparison with the low cost of the women's.[1]

Although women generally were not unwilling to cooperate with the mergers, they had important reservations. They objected to the fact that they had not been consulted when the changes were being discussed. They feared that the money they contributed to mission work with women and children would be used for other projects. Perhaps most significantly, they sensed that they were losing considerable power in the churches by giving up their executive status and by being relegated to minority committee positions and fund-raising enterprises.

In many instances, the fears of the women were well-founded. They did acquire positions on the new national mission boards, and in the Disciples of Christ they even represented 50 percent of the membership. In the Presbyterian Church, however, they became a minority voice with only fifteen of the forty seats on the Board of National and Foreign Missions. In the Presbyterian Church women also had to struggle immediately with the church's tendency to use presbytery and synod funds given by women for purposes other than missions. The mergers and subsequent protests, however, at least prompted a discussion of the status of women in several denominations. The Presbyterian Church's General Assembly even commissioned a special study of the "unrest" among the church's women.

It should be noted that the first decades of the twentieth century brought increased restrictions on the involvement of women in other groups within the Christian tradition. The Quakers, for example, abolished separate Women's Meetings and incorporated women into the Society's general meetings. The relative freedom enjoyed by many American nuns in the nineteenth century to adapt their life styles to the needs of the American environment was curtailed. Church authorities demanded that the rules governing each community be applied rigorously to the details of everyday life. Nuns were carefully cloistered and their conformity to the rules was closely monitored. They were removed from the care of babies and maternity cases in hospitals and forbidden to teach in coeducational schools. They were especially warned not to form "particular friendships" with men in the church.

The freedom found by women in the Holiness groups also diminished in the twentieth century. This was partly caused by the influence of fundamentalism which focused on a literal reading of the Bible. The Holiness groups also tried to conform more closely to the practices of the mainline denominations and American culture in general. Their desire to be acceptable and to flourish led them to discourage women preachers and to establish theological seminaries for the creation of a professional ministry. These trends greatly reduced the number of women ministers in the Holiness churches.

The 1930s brought little progress in the struggle to elevate the status of women in the Christian community and in the wider society. This stagnation can be attributed partly to the virtual disappearance of an active feminist movement in the United States.[2] The suffrage movement was successful because of the support of large numbers of women who continued to accept the Victorian ideal of true womanhood. They regarded the ballot box as a way to extend their maternal and moral influence and once that goal was reached, they retreated to kitchen and nursery. They had little interest in economic issues or in the acquisition of equality for women in the workplace. Added to this resurgence of the cult of true womanhood were the economic conditions of the 1930s. Few churches were inclined to hire women for any kind of position when so many men were competing for jobs.

POST-WAR CHANGES

Like its predecessor, World War II also created conditions that gave rise to new discussions and studies of the status of women in the Christian community. Women did many kinds of jobs that had been looked upon previously as male domains because of a shortage of available men. The Christian churches were no exception in this willingness to accept women in unusual roles. In Europe women with theological training were ordained in certain churches and became pastors in the absence of men. A shortage of men even prompted the Anglican bishop of Hong Kong to ordain Reverend Li Tim Oi to the priesthood, although her ordination was rejected by the English church hierarchy and she subsequently resigned. Events in the churches of Europe and elsewhere stimulated the American churches to examine again the status of women.

The American denominations were goaded into action by some additional factors. The 1950s saw a period of growth in church membership and building. The need for clergy and trained lay professionals made at least some leaders more open to the inclusion of women. Also, the churches were encouraged to consider the status of women by the newly formed World Council of Churches. A study of women in American religious life was conducted in preparation for the first meeting of the Council in 1948. The findings from the United States and other countries were later interpreted and published by Kathleen Bliss in a landmark book, *The Service and Status of Women in the Churches*.[3] The book documented the lowly place occupied by women in the churches and their virtual nonexistence in positions of leadership and authority.

Ordained women throughout the 1950s and 1960s continued to be few in number. Some significant changes were occurring, however, in the Protestant world. The African Methodist Episcopal Church voted to ordain women in 1948. In 1956, the Presbyterian Church in the U.S.A. ordained Margaret E. Towner as a minister in keeping with its new policy granting women full ecclesiastical privileges. After its union with this church two years later, the United Presbyterian Church of North America also acknowledged the right of women to be ordained as elders and ministers. Also in 1956, the United Methodist Church (made up of the Methodist Episcopal Church, the Methodist Protestant Church, and the Methodist Episcopal Church South) granted full conference rights to women. Seminaries such as Harvard Divinity School and Episcopal Divinity School opened their full theological programs to women.

In several denominations women served in newly created lay professional positions. Although these jobs did not entail ordination, they gave women an opportunity to do full-time church work in exchange for a salary and a degree of status. These jobs evolved before World War II at a time when congregations were concerned to hire experts or professionals in particular fields such as education, youth work, or music. These positions were open to men and women although the low pay and status made them female preserves. The Presbyterian Church in the U.S.A. formally recognized these ministries in the position of Commissioned Church Worker in 1938 and, later, the Certified Church Educator. The Lutheran church's position of Certified Lay Professional was a comparable opportunity for service.

In many cases these professional positions offered very little to women who were seeking equality and full participation in the Christian community. The salaries were usually less than half of what ordained men received, and worker benefits were often nonexistent. Women in such posts were frequently the last hired and first fired on a church staff. They had poorly defined relationships with the decision-making bodies of their denominations. They were considered church professionals yet they had no vote in running the institutions they served. Finally, they often found their tasks frustrating. Women frequently became the "errand girls" of the ordained staff, burdened with the mundane and detailed work that others did not want to do.

A New Agenda for Women

The agenda of the Christian community regarding its female members was set in the 1960s by events in American society. The Civil Rights Act of 1964, which prohibited discrimination on the grounds of sex as well as race, followed closely on the heels of a Presidential Commission that found that women were second-class citizens in almost every area of American life. During this same period books such as Betty Friedan's *The Feminine Mystique*[4] voiced the frustration and rage of women who were tired of being assigned spheres and roles and images in a society that was supposed to offer dignity and opportunity to all. The issue of the status of women in modern American society was brought before the public and a movement of radical organized feminism was launched.

Many women in the Christian community embarked upon a program of taking stock in order to evaluate their status in the churches. They discovered that although many legal barriers to full participation had been removed, women were still marginal in the professional ministry. They also became aware of the low salaries and low status of women who were lay professionals. They became aware of the small number of women in leadership positions at all levels of church life. They recognized the painful reality that the nineteenth-century image of woman as homemaker and moral guardian was still very much alive. As Beverly Harrison observes, the belief that the battle for women's rights had been won in church and society by the collapse of formal barriers was an illusion.[5]

Denominational reports and special studies were important vehicles for this self-discovery and new consciousness. An American Baptist report in 1968, for example, revealed only a small percentage of women on the church's national staff. Most of these women occupied low-level posts as administrative assistants. The number of women in upper-level jobs had actually decreased between 1958 and 1968. A year later a special report to the General Assembly of the United Presbyterian Church acknowledged that a "profound bias" against women continued to exist in the Christian community. A similar statistical study in the United Methodist Church documented the inferior status and limited roles of women, showing among other things that fewer than 1 percent of active, ordained Methodist ministers were women.

Another vehicle that acquainted women with the realities of inequality was the vast body of literature that emerged during the early 1970s on sexism in the churches. Some of this material simply described ecclesiastical inequality, making the observation that women were finding more opportunities for participation and dignity outside rather than inside the Christian community. Other publications tried to analyze the causes of sexual inequality in the churches by probing past history and the biased ways in which the biblical material had been interpreted. These publications made women aware that they were confronting images and roles that were deep-rooted in the Judeo-Christian tradition.

Women in many denominations also became conscious of their situation through formal and informal discussions with other women. From seminary lounges to church Bible study groups to preplanned gatherings such as the World Council of Church's conference on sexism in 1974, women began to share both positive and negative experiences of living and working in the Christian tradition. Like much of the literature on women, the groups were frequently ecumenical. This kind of communal experience provided some women with a chance to talk about their frustrations, learn that they were not alone, and make a start at building relationships with other women. These group gatherings would eventually provide a new setting for theology in the Christian community.

Black women as a group also began to examine their status in the Christian communities. For centuries they operated as the "glue" that held the black community together, reflecting their African heritage of economic and religious importance. In the face of profound oppression, they cared about preserving and continuing prayer, education, family life, and the programs of the churches. Yet they realized that they had been systematically excluded from positions of authority and leadership. Rosemary Radford Ruether observes that the black church has been "superpatriarchal" because only in the church did the black man find an opportunity for power which was denied to him in society at large.[6] Black women also began to resent the fact that their strength was regarded with humiliation by black men and their experiences had been ignored by black theologians.

The outcome of these exercises in self-discovery and awareness was the formation of more permanent organizations within ecclesiastical structures to seek justice for women. The American Baptist Convention, for example, formed its Executive Staff Women in 1969 to study the involvement of women in the churches and then followed this up with a Task Force on Women. A United Methodist Women's Caucus was established to promote the rights and participation of women within that denomination and in 1973 the Presbyterians organized their Council on Women and the Church to identify issues relevant to the status of women in church and society.

As Methodist historian Norma Mitchell has observed, the concerns of these organizations represent a shift from "social" to "radical" feminism in the churches.[7] "Social" feminism is the term used to describe moderate feminism which focuses on one issue such as suffrage but which accepts the ideals of true womanhood. The groups that sprang up in the latter part of the twentieth century do not focus on one particular issue but have a broad range of concerns much as the early nineteenth-century feminists did. Advocacy for a higher percentage of women on church boards and agencies is continued and women are encouraged to enter the ordained ministry. But they also urge that an end be put to male dominance in the study of the Bible and church history, in theology, and in the liturgies and hymns of worship. They focus attention on ethical issues that concern women and they encourage the critical scrutiny of traditional marriage and family relationships. What also distinguishes radical feminism from the more moderate social feminism is a sense of urgency and impatience with compromise.

Due in part to changes in the status of women in American culture and in part to the advocacy of such church organizations, the 1970s were a period of change for women in the Christian community. A short analysis of their involvement in several areas of Christian life—theological education, the ministry, theology and ethics, and liturgics—is presented in the next chapter. Not only have significant numbers of women begun to participate in all areas of church life but many women are also seeing themselves as agents of transformation. They are attempting to construct a different theology and a different style of ministry. Some of this transformation is spontaneous and unconscious, some is carefully planned and executed. Many women are certain, however, that their coming of age in the Christian community means that the present order will change and nothing will remain the same.

CHAPTER 10

AGENTS OF TRANSFORMATION

WOMEN IN THE ORDAINED MINISTRY

Some Protestant churches continue to place legal barriers in the way of women who wish to enter the ordained ministry. As late as 1984 the Southern Baptist convention passed a resolution opposing the ordination of women which, because of Baptist government, is not binding on the local congregations. The Missouri Synod Lutherans have remained firmly opposed to the ordination of women. The reasoning behind the Missouri Synod and Southern Baptist positions is still put forward by many groups in the Christian community: According to the Bible, women are to be subservient to men in church and at home as a punishment for bringing sin into the world and as an acknowledgment of their secondary status in the order of creation.

Roman Catholicism and
Eastern Orthodoxy

Most recent discussions of the ordination issue, however, have taken place in reference to the policies of the Catholic and Eastern Orthodox churches. These churches include in their membership over one-half of the Christians in the world. The refusal of the church hierarchies to ordain women has been a source of anguish for many women and an occasion to unite in advocating full participation by women in all of the church offices open to men.

Since the 1960s, Catholic women in the United States, with the support of many men, have been pressing actively for ordination to the priesthood. Although the St. Joan's International Alliance gave Catholic women an opportunity to work for the goals of feminism from the early twentieth century, the rising feminist consciousness of nuns in the 1960s raised the issue of women's rights on a large scale in the church. The powerful Leadership Conference of Women Religious made some startling assertions which led many Catholic women, married and celibate alike, to examine their status. The women of the Leadership Conference regarded themselves as "loyal dissenters" who looked to Jesus rather than the Bible, the church's hierarchy, or tradition as the authority for faith and practice. They made efforts to acquaint Catholics with the church's long history of female oppression and they urged that women participate in the decision-making bodies of the institution. They also supported the opening of all of the church's ministries to any person called by God.

In 1974 the work of the Leadership Conference bore fruit in the form of a meeting held to discuss the ordination of women to the priesthood. Scholarly studies favoring ordination were made available through the conference and a permanent staff was organized to inform interested Catholics and enlist their support.

The documents and spirit of Vatican II gave some hope to women who sought ordination. The church condemned discrimination among persons on the basis of sex and it affirmed the equality of men and women, although women were still urged to seek fulfillment as wives and mothers. In 1976, however, the Vatican made an official statement declaring that women could not be admitted to the priesthood. The statement did not say that women are inferior to men nor did it resort to ancient fears regarding the uncleanliness of women. Rather, the Vatican claimed that since the priest was the "image," "sign," and "representation" of Jesus before the people of God, a man would have to fill this role since Jesus was a male. The declaration was strongly denounced by theologians and women's groups and there is some evidence that popular support for the ordination of women increased in the United States as a result.

Theologian Paul Jewett has made a careful study of the arguments opposing the ordination of women that have circulated in the Catholic, Orthodox, and Anglican churches.[1] He outlines three main points made by the opponents of ordination. First, they often claim that a woman before the altar would distract men from the purpose of worship by arousing sexual feelings in an atmosphere already charged with emotion. Second, the point is made that the priestly office is a position of authority and leadership which cannot be granted to women who have been created as inferior to men. Finally, they frequently turn to the "maleness" of God, Jesus, and the twelve apostles to stress that women cannot act as God's representatives on earth.

The 1976 "Consultation on the Role of Orthodox Women in the Church and in Society" held in Agapia, Romania, brought together women involved in education, social work, theological study, and the monastic life and male representatives from the various church hierarchies.[2] The recommendations that emerged from the consultation were based on the belief that women have special feminine gifts which they should be encouraged to use in full partnership with men. They should, for example, have full access to theological education and be able to teach theology if qualified. The consultation also urged that the office of deacon be revived for women, complete with the ancient Eastern tradition of ordination. The participants also recommended that women be admitted to the orders of reader and acolyte and that nuns be given a voice in decisions affecting their lives. The issue of the ordination of women to the priesthood was not considered seriously by the consultation.

Protestant Churches

In November 1970, Elizabeth A. Platz became the first woman to enter the ordained ministry of the Lutheran Church in America. Her ordination was made possible when the denomination revised its constitution during its Minneapolis assembly in the summer of that same year. The constitutional change was due in no small measure to the initiative of Lutheran Church Women who had come to believe that their long-standing support of women as ministers of Christ and as capable leaders compelled them to support the ordination of women. The L.C.A., the largest Lutheran church body in North America, was the first to ordain women. That same year saw the American Lutheran Church, the second largest Lutheran church body, make the historic change to ordain women at its convention. The A.L.C., too, had ordained a woman before the end of 1970.

The Protestant Episcopal Church opened ordination to women only after a very bitter struggle. The church hierarchy first agreed to ordain women as deacons and simultaneously allowed them to become lay delegates to one of the national governing bodies, the House of Deputies. Eventually a National Committee was formed to lobby for full ordination rights. A period of upheaval in the church followed the defeat of such a resolution in 1973, and a number of women were ordained by sympathetic bishops without the sanction of the church hierarchy in 1974. Two years later women were admitted to the priesthood, although dissident bishops were allowed to refuse to ordain women or recognize them as priests if they so chose.

The number of ordained women in the mainline denominations grew rapidly in the late 1970s and early 1980s. Although they still represent less than 5 percent of all clergy, women have continued to enter the ordained ministry in larger and larger numbers. The United Church of Christ in

1981 reported the largest number of clergywomen. Theologian Letty Russell has even suggested that in the future the ordained ministry may become a "female" profession such as nursing or elementary school teaching with similar problems of low status and pay.[3]

While many women who are ordained have relatively little trouble in finding their first position, they generally discover that their career lines remain flat. They often take positions as assistants, associates, or pastors of small congregations only to find that their second, third, and subsequent jobs are much the same. In addition, women report salary inequities with male colleagues in identical situations.

Ordained women still face resistance from many groups in organized church life. Some of this resistance, on the surface at least, can be attributed to traditional views regarding the biblical commands that Christian women be silent and exercise no authority over men. Other reasons, however, have been suggested. Opposition from male clergy, for example, may be rooted in their fears that the ministry, with its emphasis on caring and its association with family life, has already become feminized in a highly technical culture.[4] The woman in the pulpit may exacerbate these fears. Also, men may view women as competitors in a shrinking job market. Sociologist Edward Lehman suggests that concern for the well-being of the church as an organization lies at the root of much resistance to clergywomen.[5] Both Baptist lay people and denominational executives interviewed by Lehman said that while they personally supported clergywomen, they had a strong perception that other people in their congregations would object to a woman, thus upsetting the harmony and stability of the organization. It is impossible at the moment to know whether or not increased exposure to clergywomen will put these kinds of objections to rest.

New Perspectives on Ministry

Women who are serving churches as ordained ministers and priests are beginning to change the weave and texture of ministry in some cases. There are very few preconceived ideas or stereotypes of what a woman minister is like, thus giving women in ministry the opportunity to do things differently. One of the most visible changes has been in the area of leadership style. Clergywomen are less inclined to see themselves as authoritarian leaders set apart in status from the lay people. Rather, they tend to see themselves as part of a ministry in which the whole church shares. They are more inclined to use the circle or rainbow as a model for ministry rather than the pyramid. They are also willing to draw out and use the resources of all members of the community, showing special sensitivity to those who have been previously shut out from meaningful participation.

Women are also contributing to a new understanding of pastoral care in the churches. Some clergywomen use the term "midwife" to describe their counseling style. Both men and women appear to regard female pastors as more approachable and less judgmental than male pastors. As a result, church members are more willing to become vulnerable by sharing themselves at a deep level. Some clergywomen in turn find that they are skilled at helping others give birth to new talent and dimensions of personality. They also often find that their social conditioning as women makes them attentive listeners, able to step over to the side of another and hear with that person's ears and see with that person's eyes.

THE MINISTRY OF DEACONESS AND NUN

The position of deaconess continues to exist in several denominations and has continued to become more professionalized. Women who enter this ministry are required to be fully trained in areas such as social work or nursing. They are also required to take courses in theology and biblical studies. The position, however, has attracted fewer and fewer women as ordination to the priesthood and ministry has become an option. The United Methodist Church has created an Office of Diaconal Ministry for men and women who minister as lay professionals in education or social work or as ministers of music in local congregations.

The years following Vatican II brought a period of turmoil and self-examination to Catholic women in religious orders. Communities began to grow smaller and the median age began to rise. Women who did not wish to become wives and mothers were offered options by secular society. Women who joined the communities in the 1960s and 1970s were often dissatisfied with the quality of community life. In some convents almost two-thirds of the new members eventually left the order. The traditional tasks of the nun in the United States—nursing and the education of immigrants—either became unnecessary or were taken over by lay professionals.

Although convent life continues to experience uncertainty and instability, some women have responded in creative ways to the new challenges. When interviewed, many of them agree that they prefer the new approaches to community life, even when long-established traditions are disrupted.

One major change has involved the question of authority in the lives of individual nuns and in the shared life of the community. In the past, the superior of the convent was regarded as the mouthpiece for the will of God. She acted as such by enforcing the community's rule. Now, however, nuns continue to speak of obedience to the will of God but they listen to their own consciences and the voice of God in prayer and the Bible as well as church authorities. They are expected to make their own decisions about life style and to take responsibility for these decisions. Often this means that even within a single community there will be several ways of dressing and many ways of working, including some outside the convent walls. Also, many communities now have no superiors and instead make decisions as a group on issues such as how money will be spent.

Some of the ancient concepts associated with the virgin life are beginning to disappear or are being reinterpreted. Nuns, for example, are less frequently seen as the brides of Christ and the ceremonies using the wedding gown and ring are fading away. Many nuns also recognize that they are not living in true poverty and strive instead to simplify their lives as much as possible. Obedience, as we have seen, now involves a large element of personal choice and responsibility. Many nuns continue to live celibate lives but they have tried not to interpret this as an indictment of sexuality. Rather they see the celibate life as a way to be free for a life of total service to others. The cloistered nature of convent life has been abolished in many situations. Members of the communities now come and go freely and many communities are open to nonmembers.

Finally, women in American religious communities are setting new agendas of concerns for themselves. They are in the midst of identifying human needs in the 1980s just as they did in the nineteenth century. Many of their efforts are now directed toward the peace movement, the elimination of hunger, and economic justice for the poor and oppressed in American society.

THEOLOGICAL EDUCATION

Since the middle of the 1970s, women have become the fastest growing constituency of accredited theological schools in the United States. In 1972 women represented only 4.7 percent of the total number of students enrolled in degree programs leading to ordination. By 1980 women represented almost 15 percent of this population. In many schools of the mainline denominations, women comprise almost half of the students studying for the Master of Divinity degree. The faculties of these schools, however, remain overwhelmingly male. Women make up a little less than 10 percent of the teaching staffs and many of these women are part-time instructors. Very few are full professors.

Historian Nancy Hardesty has outlined several ways in which seminary communities relate to women.[6] These are stages through which institutions pass, although very few schools have even begun to move in the direction of the last phase described below. Stage one occurs when a handful of women enter a school to prepare for full-time work in a church, probably on the fringe. Male students are friendly and male faculty members are paternal. The second stage is one in which a growing number of women on the campus sense their marginality both in the seminary and in the churches they are preparing to enter. They form a group or "caucus" to discuss their experiences and express their anger with their situations. Often this results in a time of hostility and resistance from male students, faculty members, and administrators.

The third stage is one into which some mainline Protestant and independent seminaries have moved. Women at this stage become a significant part of the student body and they are added to the faculty. Courses on the history of women in the church and feminist theology are added to the curriculum. Administrators and faculty members make an effort to avoid language that excludes or degrades women. Because these kinds of changes are taking place in some institutions, a significant number of women interviewed in the late 1970s described their educational experiences as affirming and favorable.

A number of women in the Christian community, however, believe that theological education must move into another phase before women can be integrated into the Christian community and their experiences taken seriously.[7] They believe that theological education, in both method and content, currently reflects the perspective of white middle-class men. Instead, they propose a model that is *holistic, integrated* and *collaborative*.

Theological education should be *holistic*. It should take seriously the fact that knowledge comes not only through the use of the mind but also through senses, feelings, and intuition. It should value poetry, dance, story, and art as much as analytical prose. Seminary education should be *integrated*. This means that the distinctions between practical subjects such as religious education and pastoral care and academic subjects such as theology and biblical studies should be eliminated. Theory and practice should be united, not only in the curriculum but also in the teacher. A person cannot adequately convey the meaning of Jeremiah, for example, without some social involvement of his or her own. Finally, these women wish to abolish the educational model in which an authoritative expert pours selected information into submissive pupils. Theological education therefore should be *collaborative* rather than competitive. They wish to discourage members of the seminary community from hoarding knowledge in order to lord it over others. They believe that research should grow out of practical needs and questions, shared freely and communicated in language understood by a wide spectrum of people.

REFORMING THE LITURGY

The worship and preaching of the Christian community has been visibly affected by the concern of women over language used for God and the people of God. The implementation of inclusive language is mentioned as a major goal by many women in seminary and the ordained ministry, even among those who do not identify themselves as feminists.

Many members of the Christian community view inclusive language as a trivial concern. A few believe that the language of Bible and liturgy has been divinely revealed and should not be tampered with. But many women point out that language has been very important in perpetuating sexism. Our current language patterns have grown out of and reflect cultures in which men ruled over women and controlled the power in society. By continuing to use this language, the church reinforces and maintains this social arrangement. Sexist attitudes are reinforced as are patterns of behavior that treat women as less than fully human. Women concerned with the language issue believe that until Christians begin to think and speak in terms of equality, this equality will never be implemented in society.

Language used for God is a fundamental part of this concern. The patriarchal context in which the biblical material developed is reflected not only in masculine pronouns for God but also in overwhelmingly masculine metaphors, such as king, father, and shepherd. No one of course would say that God is actually male. In the consciousness of people constantly hearing androcentric (male-centered) language, however, the idea takes hold that this language more adequately defines the divine. Communities soon come to believe that since God is fatherlike or husbandlike, fathers and husbands must be godlike. Women are seen as less perfect or godlike. The male becomes the norm, representing humanity as it should be. The female becomes that which is different or the "other."

Many women also believe that the use of androcentric language referring to the people of God perpetuates negative attitudes toward women. They are frustrated by the preponderance of phrases such as "brotherhood of man," "sons of God," and the "God of Abraham, Isaac, and Jacob" in worship. They do not accept the argument that this language is *generic* or intended to include both men and women because they see that in practice women have been excluded from full participation in the Christian community.

The use of words like "mankind" and masculine pronouns in liturgies and hymns sends a message that women are not important. Women are invisible in the language of the worshiping community. Upon hearing and repeating this language the idea that women have nothing to contribute is reinforced. Men continue to be suspicious of women in positions of power and authority. Women are also bombarded with the message that they are nonpersons in the churches. Women may continue to view themselves as less intelligent and less capable than men and may be reluctant to take on leadership tasks. If they do succeed in acquiring a positive self-image, women often feel resentment and alienation in a worship context that ignores them.

Many women and men therefore now advocate the elimination of masculine oriented language in church documents, liturgies, hymns, sermons, and even the biblical text. They believe that the language of the Christian community should reflect the church's belief in the dignity and equality of women and men. The process of making references to the people of God inclusive involves, for example, avoiding phrases such as "sons of God." Also, they suggest that the use of the pronoun "she" to refer to the church is not appropriate since the church by definition sees itself as a servant body in an inferior position to a masculine God.

Changes in language about God have encountered stronger resistance than changes in references to men and women. Masculine pronouns can be avoided by simply repeating the word "God" or using a variation such as "Yahweh." Churches are encouraged to use metaphors for God that reflect the full range of human experience. When male images are used, they should be paired with female. Thus, the Lord's Prayer might begin, "Our Father, Our Mother" and God might be compared not only to king and shepherd but to midwife and bakerwoman, all images with biblical grounding. Sexually neutral metaphors for God such as "rock," "fire," and "creator" can be used throughout the worship service.

Some of these recommendations have been implemented. National agencies of the Presbyterian Church, for example, have published an unofficial inclusive language edition of its Confession of 1967. Words such as "his" are replaced by "God's" and the term "men" is replaced by "all people." The 1978 *Lutheran Book of Worship* makes references to the people of God inclusive by altering the words of traditional hymns. Thus, "Good Christian Men, Rejoice" becomes "Good Christian Friends, Rejoice" and "Rise Up, O Men of God!" is changed to "Rise Up, O Saints of God!" Worship leaders who must use older hymnals have been making efforts to choose hymns that already use inclusive language (some of the oldest are the best). Bulletin inserts that revise the original words of the hymns have often been used. Tools for inclusive worship include *Women and Worship: A Guide to Non-Sexist Hymns, Prayers and Liturgy* by Sharon and Thomas Emswiler.

One of the most controversial publications dealing with the problem of religious language has been the National Council of Churches' *Inclusive Language Lectionary*, which is an effort to eliminate male bias in the three-year cycle of lectionary readings for each Sunday in the Christian year. The committee tried to get Christians to look at the Bible in a fresh light while remaining faithful to the spirit of the original text and the English cadence of the Revised Standard Version.

Some of the most straightforward and least controversial changes involve the words "man," "men," and "brethren," which were made inclusive. In many instances the NCC committee was returning to more correct translations of the Greek and Hebrew texts. In John 16:21, for example, the Greek word "man" should really be translated as "human being." More opposition, however, has been generated by changing language about Jesus. "Child of God" has been substituted for "Son of God." Jesus is called the "Human One" rather than the "Son of Man." The architects of the new readings tried to de-emphasize the idea that maleness was in any way decisive for, or a precondition of, the incarnation.

THE NEED FOR FEMINIST THEOLOGIES

Theology grows out of the experiences of a community of people with God. Yet many women have pointed out that Christian theology reflects the experiences of only one-half of the community, since it has been written and interpreted by men. It is expressed in the language and mental categories of men. As a result, it simply is not adequate for the needs and questions of women who are moving toward equality in the Christian community.

The Woman's Bible represents an early attempt to challenge male-dominated theology. In her interpretation of the parable of the wise and foolish virgins in Matthew 25, for example, the author suggests that the concept of sin must be reinterpreted to respond to the needs of women. It was meaningless to tell women that they should avoid self-interest. Woman's sin was indulging in too much self-sacrifice and not sufficient self-development. Another author suggested that a Heavenly Mother be added to the image of Heavenly Father. Yet *The Woman's Bible* and its attempts at theological reappraisal were rejected as too radical and threatening to the flourishing suffrage movement which depended on the support of church-women. It was not until the early 1970s that another such reappraisal was begun. A 1971 gathering at Alverno College in Milwaukee began an extensive process of women doing theology. The Milwaukee conference was followed by numerous others in which women began to redefine or reject the traditional mind-set of Christianity.

The involvement of women in the theological enterprise is still unfolding. Because many of the details have yet to emerge and because the theological activity of women has taken a wide variety of directions, it is possible to make only a few generalizations.

Altering Traditional Theology and Theological Methods

One point that clearly emerges from this work of women is that many have broken with traditional ways of doing theology. Women have stressed that theology should grow out of the immediate experiences of women that are shared in community. Theology is a continuing process of experience and reflection upon experience. Theology must reflect the struggle for liberation as well as the distinctively female experiences of menstruation, pregnancy, and childbirth.

Women who are doing theology may not, in some instances, be trying to create a systematic body of concepts or images with its own inner logic. Some of them object to the use of the phrase "feminist theology" to describe their work. While many women use the traditional form of analytical prose, others find this form of expression inadequate and are inclined to turn instead to stories, art, and poetry as more satisfactory vehicles of expression.

Feminist theologians have agreed that in the past Christian theology has not supported the liberation of women. A whole new framework of concepts, stories, and images must be created. Some of the basic assumptions or the "hidden agenda" of theology must be changed. One such assumption is the *dualistic* view of reality on which men have long depended. This approach places one dimension of life over against another or alienated from another rather than seeing things as a whole. Thus, God is seen as alienated from the world, male from female, mind from body, church from world, and humanity from nature.

Another problematic assumption is the *hierarchical* view of reality which traditional Christianity has often adopted. One party is in a powerful position and the other is dependent or subordinate. God is over and above humanity, the priest is over and above lay people, Christianity is over and above other religions, men are over and above women. In contrast, feminist, theologians stress equality, reciprocity, and mutuality.

Specific images, stories, and concepts within the traditional framework of Christianity subvert the full equality and dignity of women. We have already touched on many of these stories and images in our survey of Christian history. God is seen as Father, the incarnation of God was in the male Jesus, and the story telling of the origin of sin in the world places the blame on women. Mary, the ideal Christian woman, is sexless and submissive. Women regard certain common theological concepts as repressive. The idea that Christians must obey the will of God, for example, has often been used to force women to do the bidding of men. The notion of rewards in heaven has led women to accept their situation in this life with meekness. And the belief that self-sacrifice is righteous has inhibited women from developing their own talents.

In deciding how to regard traditional Christianity in the process of doing theology, women reach markedly different conclusions. Some women are led to reject the tradition, others to reform it. Some take a "revolutionary" position in declaring that Christianity in its images, concepts, and stories is hopelessly sexist and only serves the interests of a society or institution that oppresses women. These women believe that a whole new religion must be constructed in which women "name" reality for themselves. Mary Daly is a widely known representative of this position. She believes that new images, concepts, and stories to replace the old will eventually come out of the feminist experience. She has taken some steps herself toward this reconstruction by suggesting that God no longer be thought of as a "noun" (a specific being) but as a "verb," as an active power or force which women feel within themselves. This view also enables her to speak of incarnation not as something that occurred in the first-century man Jesus but as something that happens in all women.

Rosemary Radford Ruether has taken the position that the traditional biblical canon is so thoroughly sexist that women must move beyond it in order to construct a meaningful theology. She does admit that traces of female power and affirmation can be found in the biblical material. In *Womanguides: Readings Toward a Feminist Theology*, however, she finds it imperative to add to these a wide variety of texts from marginal, unorthodox Christian communities which reflect "questionings of male domination in groups where women did enter into critical dialogue." These texts can be the beginning of a "new community, a new theology, a new canon."[8]

Women such as Elisabeth Schüssler Fiorenza and Letty Russell believe that it is necessary to liberate traditional Christianity from its sexism. They believe that through reform and reinterpretation of the tradition the images, concepts, and stories can be humanized and thus claimed by women as well as men.

The model or guide for the reformist approach to Christian theology is a body of writing known as liberation theology. Liberation theology has grown out of the experiences of particular groups as they seek justice and full human rights in many social contexts. Liberation theology began in Latin America. Black and feminist theology are similar theological movements.

An understanding of some of the characteristics of liberation theology sheds light on the nature of what is being done by women. Liberation theology links reflection on God and the world with concrete social action in the world. It emphasizes stories of liberation in the Scriptures, such as the exodus. It stresses the image of "Christ the Liberator" who brings not only individual salvation but a just society. It applies the concept of sin not only to the private lives of individuals but to social structures and institutions that alienate and exploit others. It defines the task of the Christian community as participation in the struggle for the liberation of oppressed people.

Women working to reform theology have adopted many concepts, images, and stories from liberation theology. The oppression of women must be seen as only one form of oppression which has resulted from a false "naming" of reality as dualistic and hierarchical. Women must see that their situation is intimately linked or "interstructured" with that of black people, Third World countries, and low-paid workers throughout the world. Women doing theology believe that the man-woman relationship as oppressor-oppressed is very important not only because it is nearly universal but because it has provided the blueprint for other kinds of oppression throughout history.

Reformist women in theology have made a start at reinterpreting some of the stories, concepts, and images which form the core of the Christian faith. We have already explored the reinterpretation of stories such as the Genesis account of the creation and the Fall in chapter 1. This kind of exercise is an important part of women doing theology. Many of the stories of the life of Jesus have also been reinterpreted by women. His primary image becomes that of Liberator. He is one who challenges the idea that a male religious elite can "lord it over" the poor and women.

God is understood in this reinterpretation process not as an elderly father and judge over and above the world who doles out rewards and punishments. Rather, the *immanence* or indwelling of God in the universe is stressed. The image of God as Father is exchanged for the image of God as Spirit or as the Ground of our Being and both the male and female aspects of God's nature are emphasized.

Concepts and images important to the life of the church are also being reinterpreted in light of the experiences of women. "Diakonia" or service to the church is no longer defined as passive subservience but as the claiming of power and authority. The laying on of hands, according to Letty Russell, should not be used to create an authoritarian ordained elite but should be used for anyone who has a calling and an ability to perform a particular service.

Finally, because what is valued as good and right in Christianity is closely connected with theological views, the work of women in theology has influenced their ethical positions. They are inclined to reject any ethic built on a hierarchical and dualistic view of reality. They reject behavior that sees other people or the natural world as "things" to be subjugated. They reject the idea that there is one set of rules for private life and one set for public life. They place little value on physical aggression, valor, or competition and instead emphasize the need for compassion and cooperation. They tend to be concerned with the immediate and concrete results of behavior rather than with abstract ethical principles. And they have indicted the Christian community for its silence not only on issues such as rape and wife-abuse and sexual harassment (which are based on the view of women as subordinate objects) but also for its compliance with an industrial-military complex that threatens the peace and harmony of the natural and human worlds.

CONCLUSION

The past movement of women toward equality and full participation has not been one of constant progress. Rather, equality and full participation have been approximated at various times throughout Christian history only to be followed by periods of repression and retrenchment. The openness of the earliest Christian communities, for example, was followed by a return to custom and subordination. The relative freedom of women in the early monasteries was followed by an erosion of power and a move toward total cloistering. The era of mission leadership, *The Woman's Bible*, and growing professional participation in the early twentieth century was followed by a time of few institutional changes and a resurgence of the Victorian cult of true womanhood.

Since the 1960s women have made great strides toward claiming a place for themselves in the institutional churches and in the community of biblical scholars and theologians. But there are few signs that the Orthodox and Roman Catholic stance against ordination will be changed in the near future. In the Protestant denominations, women continue to enter the ministry in large numbers. Many continue to fill the pulpits of small churches or remain as junior members of church staffs, although a few are assuming senior pastoral roles. However, biblical literalism and traditional views of the role of women have touched many churches, making it more difficult for them to accept a woman as pastor.

The gains women have made have been real and significant. Changes in language and in the mind-set of Christianity have taken place in many theological seminaries, national church boards, and some congregations. The increased institutional visibility of women and their scholarly endeavors have set in motion certain forces within the Christian community which show signs of shaping the future in some surprising ways.

As we have already seen, an important part of the move toward full equality and participation for women in the churches has been critical exploration of the past. There is now a flood of writing on the history of women. There is a need for this material to be integrated into what until now has been considered mainstream church history. There is a growing recognition that women's history is relational. Men increasingly realize that women have made significant contributions to the Christian community and women are deriving inspiration from past female role models whose courage and single-minded pursuit of what they perceived as God's way enabled them to transcend cultural barriers. Women at the same time recognize that they have been affected profoundly by the events and attitudes of the entire community in the past and that they cannot study history in isolation from this total picture. It is possible that the study of women's history will provoke a new appreciation for the entire history of the Christian tradition, which for so long has been of little interest or concern to many members of the Christian churches.

A final observation I want to make is that the movement of women into the institutional leadership of the churches and into theological and biblical scholarship might serve as the vehicle for both new life in the ecumenical movement and for a recovery of the church's prophetic voice in Western culture. The theological reflection of women today and their consciousness-raising in the early 1970s have grown out of groups that include Catholic and Protestant women as well as representatives from traditions as diverse as Episcopalian and Pentecostal. These women saw and continue to see themselves as sharing a common history. They freely support each other in efforts to explore the past and change the future. A large portion of the scholarship this book utilizes comes from the pens of women with very diverse interpretations of the Christian gospel.

The Christian community is often accused of acting as the guardian rather than the critic of modern Western values. It often appears to reinforce society's emphasis on material prosperity, its tendency to see people as objects to be manipulated, and its alienation from the natural world. The church frequently seems to stand by in silence while God's created order is abused.

Throughout the history of the church, women have been agents of change, makers of history. It is possible that the stirring of women at all levels of church life will help the community as a whole to evaluate more critically the values of Western culture. Women have spoken out against the rape of the natural world, dependence on weapons of destruction, economic injustice, and the valuing of people solely on the basis of their power or economic productivity. They will continue to speak. Women have been supported in the past by the tales of justice, equality, and dignity that shine through the biblical and historical traditions, however dimly. They will continue to find reassurance in the communion of saints as well as from each other. Their interests and concerns, if heard, may set a new agenda for the entire Christian community.

NOTES

Introduction

1. Kathryn Kish Sklar, "The Last Fifteen Years," in *Women in New Worlds: Historical Perspectives on the Wesleyan Tradition*, ed. Hilah F. Thomas and Rosemary Skinner Keller (Nashville: Abingdon Press, 1981), 1:49–58.

2. Feminist interpretation of the Bible has divided in the same manner. Some women have concluded that the Bible is so thoroughly patriarchal that it cannot be used by women as the basis for theology or as a guide to life. Others claim that while the Bible has been influenced by patriarchal cultures, there is a thread of material running through the books that challenges and condemns patriarchy.

3. Eleanor McLaughlin, "The Christian Past: Does It Hold a Future for Women?" in *Womanspirit Rising: A Feminist Reader in Religion*, ed. Carol P. Christ and Judith Plaskow (San Francisco: Harper & Row, 1979), 96.

Chapter 1

1. See Phyllis Bird, "Images of Women in the Old Testament," in *Religion and Sexism: Images of Woman in the Jewish and Christian Traditions*, ed. Rosemary Radford Ruether (New York: Simon & Schuster, 1974), 41–88.

2. Quoted in Leonard Swidler, *Biblical Affirmations of Woman* (Philadelphia: Westminster Press, 1979), 155.

3. Phyllis Trible, *God and the Rhetoric of Sexuality* (Philadelphia: Fortress Press, 1978), 173.

4. This is discussed in Swidler, *Biblical Affirmations of Woman*, 29–30.

5. See, e.g., Phyllis Trible, "Good Tidings of Great Joy: Biblical Faith Without Sexism," *Christianity and Crisis* 34 (4 February 1974): 12–14; idem, *God and the Rhetoric of Sexuality*, 72–143; Katherine Doob Sakenfeld, "The Bible and Women: Bane or Blessing?" *Theology Today* 32 (October 1975): 222–26; Swidler, *Biblical Affirmations of Woman*, 75–85.

6. Trible, "Good Tidings of Great Joy," 12; idem, *God and the Rhetoric of Sexuality*, 94–105. For a different view, see Sakenfeld, "Bible and Women," 224.

7. Tertullian, "On the Apparel of Women," trans. S. Thelwall, in *The Ante-Nicene Fathers: Translations of the Writings of the Fathers Down to A.D. 325*, ed.

Alexander Roberts and James Donaldson (Buffalo: Christian Literature Pub. Co., 1885), 4:14–15.

8. Trible, "Good Tidings of Great Joy," 15–16; idem, *God and the Rhetoric of Sexuality*, 144–65.

9. For a discussion of the attitudes of Jesus toward women see Swidler, *Biblical Affirmations of Woman*, 163–218; idem, "Jesus Was a Feminist," *Southeast Asia Journal of Theology* 13 (1971): 102–10.

10. Raymond E. Brown, "Roles of Women in the Fourth Gospel," *Theological Studies* 36 (December 1975): 694.

11. For a discussion of current views on Paul see, e.g., Constance Parvey, "The Theology and Leadership of Women in the New Testament," in *Religion and Sexism: Images of Woman in the Jewish and Christian Traditions*, ed. Rosemary Radford Ruether (New York: Simon & Schuster, 1974), 123–37; Elisabeth Schüssler Fiorenza, "Women in the Pre-Pauline and Pauline Churches," *Union Seminary Quarterly Review* 33 (Spring/Summer 1978): 153–66; Barbara Hall, "Paul and Women," *Theology Today* 31 (April 1974): 50–55; Robin Scroggs, "Paul and the Eschatological Woman," *Journal of the American Academy of Religion* 40 (September 1972): 283–303; Rosemary Radford Ruether, "The Subordination and Liberation of Women in Christian Theology: St. Paul and Sarah Grimké," *Soundings* 51 (1978): 168–81.

12. Ruether, "Subordination and Liberation of Women in Christian Theology," 172.

CHAPTER 2

1. For a discussion of feminist interpretation of the New Testament as well as the activities of women, see, e.g., Elisabeth Schüssler Fiorenza, *Bread Not Stone: The Challenge of Feminist Biblical Interpretation* (Boston: Beacon Press, 1984); idem, *In Memory of Her* (New York: Crossroad, 1983); idem, "Women in the New Testament," *New Catholic World* 219 (November/December 1976): 256–60.

2. Parvey, "Theology and Leadership of Women in the New Testament," 138.

3. See, e.g., Winsome Munro, "Patriarchy and Charismatic Community in 'Paul,'" in *Women and Religion: Papers of the Working Group on Women and Religion, 1972–73*, rev. ed., ed. Judith Plaskow and Joan Arnold Romero (Missoula, Mont.: American Academy of Religion and Scholars' Press, 1974), 189.

4. Lloyd Patterson, "Women in the Early Church: A Problem of Perspective," in *Toward a New Theology of Ordination: Essays on the Ordination of Women*, ed. Marianne H. Micks (Somerville, Mass.: Greeno, Hadden & Co., 1976), 30.

5. Parvey, "Theology and Leadership of Women in the New Testament," 118–19, 136; Munro, "Patriarchy and Charismatic Community in 'Paul,'" 197–98.

6. Quoted in William Phipps, "The Menstrual Taboo in the Judaeo-Christian Tradition," *Journal of Religion and Health* 19 (Winter 1980): 300.

7. Hamilton Hess, "Changing Forms of Ministry in the Early Church," in *Sexism and Church Law*, ed. James A. Corriden (New York: Paulist Press, 1977), 55.

8. *Constitutions of the Holy Apostles*, ed. James Donaldson, in *The Ante-Nicene Fathers: Translations of the Writings of the Fathers Down to A.D. 325*, ed. Alexander Roberts and James Donaldson (Buffalo: Christian Literature Pub. Co., 1886), 7:492.

9. Quoted in Roger Gryson, *The Ministry of Women in the Early Church* (Collegeville, Minn.: Liturgical Press, 1976), 65.

10. Edgar Hennecke and Wilhelm Schneemelcher, eds., *New Testament Apocrypha*, vol. 1, *Gospels and Related Writings* (Philadelphia: Westminster Press, 1963), 256–57.

11. Reproduced in Patricia Wilson-Kastner et. al., *A Lost Tradition: Women Writers of the Early Church* (Washington, D.C.: University Press of America, 1981), 19–32.

12. This interpretation of Perpetua's writings is found in Wilson-Kastner, *Lost Tradition*, 1–12.

13. Ibid., 22.

14. Ibid., 19–20.

15. Reproduced in ibid., 45–68; 85–132.

16. Ibid., 107.

CHAPTER 3

1. Joan Morris, *The Lady Was a Bishop: The History of Women with Clerical Ordination and the Jurisdiction of Bishops* (New York: Macmillan Co., 1973), 100–104.

2. See Eleanor McLaughlin, "Women, Power and the Pursuit of Holiness," in *Women of Spirit: Female Leadership in the Jewish and Christian Traditions*, ed. Rosemary Radford Ruether and Eleanor McLaughlin (New York: Simon & Schuster, 1979), 100–130.

3. Quoted in Eleanor McLaughlin, "Equality of Souls, Inequality of Sexes," in *Religion and Sexism*, ed. Ruether, 242.

4. McLaughlin, "Women, Power and the Pursuit of Holiness," 102.

5. McLaughlin, "Equality of Souls, Inequality of Sexes," 234–35.

6. This cluster of ideas and stories is examined in detail in Marina Warner, *Alone of All Her Sex: The Myth and Cult of the Virgin Mary* (New York: Alfred A. Knopf, 1976); and Rosemary Radford Ruether, *Mary—The Feminine Face of the Church* (Philadelphia: Westminster Press, 1977).

7. This question is raised, e.g., in McLaughlin, "Equality of Souls, Inequality of Sexes," 245–51.

8. Warner, *Alone of All Her Sex*, 284.

9. For a discussion of the elements contributing to the popular conception of a witch, see Jeffrey Russell, *A History of Witchcraft* (London: Thames & Hudson, 1980), 41–42.

10. See Russell, *History of Witchcraft*, 113; Rosemary Radford Ruether, "Persecution of Witches: A Case of Ageism and Sexism?" *Christianity and Crisis* 34 (23 December 1974): 291; Clarke Garrett, "Women and Witches: Patterns of Analysis," *Signs: Journal of Women in Culture and Society* 3 (Winter 1977): 461–63.

11. *Webster's New Collegiate Dictionary* (Springfield, Mass.: G. & C. Merriam Co., 1979), 1336.

12. Ruether, "Persecution of Witches," 291; Garrett, "Women and Witches," 462–65.

13. Reginald Scot, *The Discoverie of Witchcraft* (1584; reprint, Totowa, N.J.: Rowman & Littlefield, 1973), 5.

14. Ruether, "Persecution of Witches," 292–95; Russell, *History of Witchcraft*, 113–15.

15. Julian of Norwich, *The Revelations of Divine Love*, trans. James Walsh (New York: Harper & Row, 1961), 166–67.

16. Caroline Walker Bynum, *Jesus as Mother: Studies in the Spirituality of the High Middle Ages* (Berkeley and Los Angeles: Univ. of California Press, 1982).

17. Quoted in Bynum, *Jesus as Mother*, 225.

CHAPTER 4

1. For a discussion of this see David Steinmetz, "Theological Reflections on the Reformation and the Status of Women," *Duke Divinity Review* 41 (Fall 1976): 197–207; Miriam U. Chrisman, "Women and the Reformation in Strasbourg 1490–1530," *Archive for Reformation History* 63 (1972): 142–67; Jane Dempsey Douglass, "Women and the Continental Reformation," in *Religion and Sexism*, ed. Ruether, 292–302.

2. Quoted in Chrisman, "Women and the Reformation in Strasbourg 1490–1530," 157.

3. Martin Luther, "The Misuse of the Mass," in *Luther's Works: Word and Sacrament II*, ed. Abdel R. Wentz and Helmut T. Lehman, (Philadelphia: Fortress Press, 1959), 36:152.

4. Douglass, "Women and the Continental Reformation," 297.

5. For this interpretation of Calvin see Willis DeBoer, "Calvin on the Role of Women," in *Exploring the Heritage of John Calvin* (Grand Rapids: Baker Book House, 1976), 236–72; Jane Dempsey Douglass, "Christian Freedom: What Calvin Learned at the School of Women," *Church History* 53 (June 1984): 155–73.

6. Ruth P. Liebowitz, "Virgins in the Service of Christ: The Dispute Over an Active Apostolate for Women During the Counter-Reformation," in *Women of Spirit*, ed. Ruether and McLaughlin (New York: Simon & Schuster, 1979), 146–47.

7. Douglass, "Women and the Continental Reformation," 309–14.

8. Quoted in Roland H. Bainton, *Women of the Reformation: In Germany and Italy* (Minneapolis: Augsburg Pub. House, 1971), 55.

9. Quoted in ibid., 100.

10. Joyce L. Irwin, *Womanhood in Radical Protestantism, 1525–1675* (New York: Edwin Mellen Press, 1979), 203.

CHAPTER 5

1. Anne Bradstreet, "The Tenth Muse Lately Sprung Up in America," in *The Works of Anne Bradstreet in Prose and Verse*, ed. John Harvard Ellis (Gloucester, Mass.: Peter Smith, 1962), 101.

2. James Kendall Hosmer, ed., *Winthrop's Journal: History of New England 1630–1649* (New York: Charles Scribner's Sons, 1908), 2:225.

3. Cotton Mather, *Ornaments for the Daughters of Zion or The Character and Happiness of a Virtuous Woman*, facsimile reproduction with an introduction by Pattie Cowell (Delmar, N.Y.: Scholars' Facsimiles and Reprints, 1978), 1–2.

4. See Amanda Porterfield, *Feminine Spirituality in America* (Philadelphia: Temple Univ. Press, 1970), 34; Margaret Masson, "The Typology of the Female as a

Model for the Regenerate: Puritan Preaching 1690–1730," *Signs: Journal of Women in Culture and Society* 2 (Winter 1976), 310.

5. Page Smith, *Daughters of the Promised Land: Women in American History* (Boston: Little, Brown & Co., 1970), 35.

6. Hosmer, *Winthrop's Journal*, 1:299.

7. David D. Hall, ed., *Antinomian Controversy, 1636–1638: A Documentary History* (Middletown, Conn.: Wesleyan Univ. Press, 1968), 312.

8. See Lyle Koehler, "The Case of the American Jezebels: Anne Hutchinson and Female Agitation During the Years of Antinomian Turmoil, 1636–1640," in *Our Sisters: Women in American Life and Thought*, ed. Jean Friedman and William Shade (Boston: Allyn & Bacon, 1976); Carol V. R. George, "Anne Hutchinson and the Revolution Which Never Happened," in *Remember the Ladies: New Perspectives on Women in American History*, ed. Carol V. R. George (Syracuse, N.Y.: Syracuse Univ. Press, 1975).

9. Quoted in Stephen Stein, "A Note on Anne Dutton, Eighteenth Century Evangelical," *Church History* 44 (December 1975): 487.

10. Ibid., 491.

11. Mary Beth Norton, "'My Resting Reaping Times': Sarah Osborn's Defense of Her 'Unfeminine' Activities," *Signs: Journal of Women in Culture and Society* 2 (Winter 1976): 515–29.

12. Ibid., 527.

13. Sereno Edwards Dwight, *The Life of President Edwards* (New York: G & C. & H. Carvill, 1830), 178.

14. Porterfield, *Feminine Spirituality in America*, 47.

15. Quoted in Julia Spruill, *Women's Life and Work in the Southern Colonies* (Chapel Hill, N.C.: Univ. of North Carolina Press, 1938; reprint, New York: Norton and Co., 1972), 253.

CHAPTER 6

1. Barbara Welter, "The Cult of True Womanhood, 1820–1860," in *Dimity Convictions: The American Woman in the Nineteenth Century* (Athens: Ohio Univ. Press, 1976), 21–41. See also Janet Forsythe Fishburn, *The Fatherhood of God and the Victorian Family: The Social Gospel in America* (Philadelphia: Fortress Press, 1981), passim.

2. See, e.g., Mary P. Ryan, *Womanhood in America from Colonial Times to the Present*, 3d ed. (New York: Franklin Watts, 1983), 118; Barbara Harris, *Beyond Her Sphere: Women and the Professions in American History* (Westport, Conn.: Greenwood Press, 1978), 56–57.

3. Welter, "The Cult of True Womanhood, 1820–1860," 21.

4. This is discussed in Barbara Welter, "The Feminization of American Religion, 1800–1860," in *Dimity Convictions*, 83–102; Ann Douglas, *The Feminization of American Culture* (New York: Alfred A. Knopf, 1977).

5. Quoted in R. Pierce Beaver, *American Protestant Women in World Mission: History of the First Feminist Movement in North America*, rev. ed. (Grand Rapids: Wm. B. Eerdmans, 1980), 46.

6. Keith Melder, "Ladies Bountiful: Organized Women's Benevolence in Early Nineteenth Century America," *New York History* 48 (July 1967): 249; Nancy Cott,

The Bonds of Womanhood: Woman's Sphere in New England 1780–1835 (New Haven, Conn.: Yale Univ. Press, 1977), 138.

7. Lydia Maria Child, "Speaking in the Church," *The National Anti-Slavery Standard* 2 (15 July, 1841): 22.

8. For a discussion of this issue see Blanche Glassman Hersh, *The Slavery of Sex: Feminist Abolitionists in America* (Urbana: Univ. of Illinois Press, 1978), 1–5; Cott, *The Bonds of Womanhood*, 156; Melder, "Ladies Bountiful," 249–50; Harris, *Beyond Her Sphere*, 73–90; Ryan, *Womanhood in America from Colonial Times to the Present*, 132–34.

9. Beverly Wildung Harrison, "Early Feminists and the Clergy: A Case Study in the Dynamics of Secularization," *Review and Expositor* 72 (Winter 1975): 47.

10. Beaver, *American Protestant Women in World Mission*, 54.

11. Lucy H. Daggett, *Historical Sketches of Woman's Missionary Societies in America and England* (Boston: Mrs. L. H. Daggett, 1879), 106.

12. Barbara Welter, "She Hath Done What She Could: Protestant Women's Missionary Careers in Nineteenth Century America," in *Women in American Religion*, ed. Janet Wilson James (Philadelphia: Univ. of Pennsylvania Press, 1980), 125.

13. Ibid., 123.

14. Beverly Wildung Harrison, "Sexism and the Contemporary Church: When Evasion Becomes Complicity," in *Sexist Religion and Women in the Church: No More Silence!*, ed. Alice Hageman (New York: Association Press, 1974), 203.

CHAPTER 7

1. Martha Tomhave Blauvelt, "Women and Revivalism," in *Women and Religion in America*, vol. 1, *The Nineteenth Century*, ed. Rosemary Radford Ruether and Rosemary Skinner Keller (San Francisco: Harper & Row, 1981), 3–4; Nancy Cott, "Young Women in the Second Great Awakening in New England," *Feminist Studies* 3 (1975): 18–19.

2. Donald W. Dayton and Lucille Sider Dayton, "Women as Preachers: Evangelical Precedents," *Christianity Today* 19 (23 May 1975): 4.

3. Quoted in Lucille Sider Dayton and Donald W. Dayton, "'Your Daughters Shall Prophesy': Feminism in the Holiness Movement," *Methodist History* 14 (January 1976): 84.

4. Catherine Booth, *Female Ministry: or, Woman's Right to Preach the Gospel* (London: 1859; reprint, New York: Salvation Army, 1975), 14.

5. Seth C. Rees, *The Ideal Pentecostal Church* (Cincinnati: M. W. Knapp, 1897), 41.

6. These are discussed in detail in Barbara Brown Zikmund, "The Struggle for the Right to Preach," in *Women and Religion in America*, vol. 1, *The Nineteenth Century*, ed. Ruether and Keller, 193–241.

7. Stephen Knowlton, "The Silence of Women in the Churches," *Congregational Quarterly* 9 (October 1867): 332.

8. Virginia Brereton and Christa Klein, "American Women in Ministry: A History of Protestant Beginning Points," in *Women in American Religion*, ed. Janet Wilson James (Philadelphia: Univ. of Pennsylvania Press, 1980), 179–80.

9. *The Woman's Bible*, Part I, Comments on Genesis, Exodus, Leviticus, Num-

bers and Deuteronomy (New York: European Pub. Co., 1892; reprint, New York: Arno Press, 1972), 117.

10. Ibid., 14.

CHAPTER 8

1. Mary Ewens, "Removing the Veil: The Liberated American Nun," in *Women of Spirit: Female Leadership in the Jewish and Christian Traditions*, ed. Ruether and McLaughlin, 256–78; idem, *The Role of the Nun in Nineteenth Century America* (New York: Arno Press, 1978).

2. James Keneally, "Eve, Mary and the Historians: American Catholicism and Women," in *Women in American Religion*, ed. James, 190–206.

3. Ewens, "Removing the Veil," 256–57.

4. Quoted in Charles Nordhoff, *The Communistic Societies of the United States: From Personal Visit and Observation: Including Detailed Accounts of the Economists, Zoarites, Shakers, the Amana, Oneida, Bethel, Aurora, Icarian, and Other Existing Societies, Their Religious Creeds, Social Practices, Numbers, Industries and Present Condition* (New York: Harper & Brothers, 1875), 125.

5. See D'Ann Campbell, "Woman's Life in Utopia: The Shaker Experiment in Sexual Equality Reappraised 1810–1860," *New England Quarterly* 51 (March 1978): 23–38.

6. See Barbara Brown Zikmund, "The Feminist Thrust of Sectarian Christianity," in *Women of Spirit: Female Leadership in the Jewish and Christian Traditions*, ed. Ruether and McLaughlin, 206–24.

7. See, e.g., Margery Fox, "Protest in Piety: Christian Science Revisited," *International Journal of Women's Studies* 1 (July/August 1978): 412–13.

8. Laurence Moore, "Spiritualist Medium: A Study of Female Professionalism in Victorian America," *American Quarterly* 27 (May 1975): 207.

CHAPTER 9

1. Beaver, *American Protestant Women in World Mission*, 180–82.

2. See Harris, *Beyond Her Sphere*, 127–46.

3. Kathleen Bliss, *The Service and Status of Women in the Churches* (London: SCM Press, 1952).

4. Betty Friedan, *The Feminine Mystique* (New York: Norton, 1963).

5. Harrison, "Sexism and the Contemporary Church," 206.

6. Rosemary Radford Ruether, "Crisis in Sex and Race: Black Theology vs. Feminist Theology," *Christianity and Crisis* 34 (15 April, 1974): 69.

7. Norma Mitchell, "From Social to Radical Feminism: A Survey of Emerging Diversity in Methodist Women's Organizations, 1869–1974," *Methodist History* 13 (April 1975): 33.

CHAPTER 10

1. Paul Jewett, *The Ordination of Women* (Grand Rapids: Wm. B. Eerdmans, 1980).

2. See *Orthodox Women: Their Role and Participation in the Orthodox Church*, Re-

port on the Consultation of Orthodox Women, 11–17 September, 1976, Agapia, Romania. (Agapia, Romania: World Council of Churches, Subunit on Women in Church and Society, 1976).

3. "Women Clergy: How Their Presence Is Changing the Church: A Symposium by Five Women on the Seminary Campus," *Christian Century* 96 (7 February 1979): 125. Letty Russell's section is subtitled "Clerical Ministry as a Female Profession."

4. This question is discussed in Jackson Carroll et al., *Women of the Cloth: New Opportunity for the Churches* (New York: Harper & Row, 1983), 41–42.

5. Edward Lehman, "Organizational Resistance to Women in Ministry," *Sociological Analysis: A Journal in the Sociology of Religion* 42 (Summer 1981): 101–18.

6. "Women Clergy: How Their Presence Is Changing the Church," p. 122. Nancy Hardesty's contribution is subtitled "Women and the Seminaries."

7. This perspective is most fully represented in Cornwall Collective, *Your Daughters Shall Prophesy: Feminist Alternatives in Theological Education* (New York: Pilgrim Press, 1980).

8. Rosemary Radford Ruether, *Womanguides: Readings Toward a Feminist Theology* (Boston: Beacon Press, 1985), x–xi.

SUGGESTIONS FOR FURTHER READING

INTRODUCTION

Bass, Dorothy. *American Women in Church and Society 1607–1920: A Bibliography.* New York: Auburn Theological Seminary, 1973.

Carroll, Bernice, ed. *Liberating Women's History: Theoretical and Critical Essays.* Urbana: Univ. of Illinois Press, 1976.

Christ, Carol P. "The New Feminist Theology: A Review of the Literature." *Religious Studies Review* 3 (October 1977): 203–12.

———. "Women's Studies in Religion." *Bulletin of the Council for the Study of Religion* 10 (February 1979): 3–5.

Clark, Elizabeth, and Herbert Richardson. *Women and Religion: A Feminist Sourcebook of Christian Thought.* New York: Harper & Row, 1977.

Culver, Elsie T. *Women in the World of Religion.* Garden City, N.Y.: Doubleday & Co., 1967.

Driver, Anne Barstow. "Review Essay: Religion." *Signs: Journal of Women in Culture and Society* 2 (Winter 1976): 434–42.

Frazier, Ruth F., ed. *Women and Religion: A Bibliography Selected from the ATLA Religion Database.* 3d rev. ed. Chicago: American Theological Library Association, 1983.

James, Edward T., Janet Wilson James, and Paul S. Boyer, eds. *Notable American Women 1607–1950: A Biographical Dictionary.* 3 vols. Cambridge, Mass.: Belknap Press of Harvard Univ. Press, 1971.

Kelly-Gadol, Joan. "The Social Relation of the Sexes: Methodological Implications of Women's History." *Signs: Journal of Women in Culture and Society* 1 (Summer 1976): 809–23.

Lerner, Gerda. *The Majority Finds Its Past: Placing Women in History.* New York & London: Oxford Univ. Press, 1979.

Mead, Judith, comp. *Resource List.* New York: Council on Women and the Church (Presbyterian Church [U.S.A.]), 1983.

O'Faolain, Julia, and Laura Martines. *Not in God's Image: Women in History from the Greeks to the Victorians.* New York: Harper & Row, 1973.

Patrick, Anne E., "Women and Religion: A Survey of Significant Literature, 1965–1974." *Theological Studies* 36 (December 1975): 737–65.

Sicherman, Barbara, Carol Hurd Green, Ilene Kantrov, and Hariette Walker, eds. *Notable American Women: The Modern Period: A Biographical Dictionary.* Cambridge, Mass.: Belknap Press of Harvard Univ. Press, 1980.

Sklar, Kathryn Kish. "The Last Fifteen Years." In *Women in New Worlds: Historical Perspectives on the Wesleyan Tradition.* Vol. 1. Edited by Hilah F. Thomas and Rosemary Skinner Keller. Nashville: Abingdon Press, 1981.

CHAPTER 1

Bass, Dorothy C. "Women's Studies and Biblical Studies: An Historical Perspective." *Journal for the Study of the Old Testament* 22 (1982): 6–12.

Bird, Phyllis. "Images of Women in the Old Testament." In *Religion and Sexism: Images of Woman in the Jewish and Christian Traditions*, edited by Rosemary Radford Ruether, 41–88. New York: Simon & Schuster, 1974.

Brooten, Bernadette. "Feminist Perspectives on New Testament Exegesis." In *Conflicting Ways of Interpreting the Bible*, edited by Hans Küng, 55–61. Concilium Religion in the Eighties, vol. 138. New York: Seabury Press, 1980.

Brown, Raymond. "Roles of Women in the Fourth Gospel." *Theological Studies* 36 (December 1975): 688–99.

Collins, Adela Yarbro. "New Testament Perspectives: The Gospel of John." *Journal for the Study of the Old Testament* 22 (1982): 47–53.

Fiorenza, Elisabeth Schüssler. *Bread Not Stone: The Challenge of Feminist Biblical Interpretation.* Boston: Beacon Press, 1984.

_____. "Feminist Theology and New Testament Interpretation." *Journal for the Study of the Old Testament* 22 (1982): 32–46.

_____. *In Memory of Her.* New York: Crossroad, 1983.

_____. "Women in the New Testament." *New Catholic World* 219 (November/December 1976): 256–60.

_____. "Women in the Pre-Pauline and Pauline Churches." *Union Seminary Quarterly Review* 33 (Spring/Summer 1978): 153–66.

_____. "'You Are Not to Be Called Father': Early Christian History in a Feminist Perspective." In *The Bible and Liberation: Political and Social Hermeneutics*, edited by Norman K. Gottwald, 394–417. Revised edition of *A Radical Religion Reader.* Maryknoll, N.Y.: Orbis Books, 1983.

Hall, Barbara. "Paul and Women." *Theology Today* 31 (April 1974): 50–55.

Hamerton-Kelly, Robert. *God the Father: Theology and Patriarchy in the Teaching of Jesus.* Overtures to Biblical Theology 4. Philadelphia: Fortress Press, 1979.

Higgins, Jean M. "The Myth of Eve: The Temptress." *Journal of the American Academy of Religion* 44 (December 1976): 639–47.

Mollenkott, Virginia. *The Divine Feminine: The Biblical Imagery of God as Female.* New York: Crossroad, 1983.

_____. *Women, Men and the Bible.* Nashville: Abingdon Press, 1977.

Pagels, Elaine H. "Paul and Women: A Response to Recent Discussion." *Journal of the American Academy of Religion* 42 (September 1974): 538–49.

Parvey, Constance. "The Theology and Leadership of Women in the New Testament." In *Religion and Sexism: Images of Woman in the Jewish and Christian Traditions*, edited by Rosemary Radford Ruether, 117–49. New York: Simon &

Schuster, 1974.

Ruether, Rosemary Radford. "Feminism and Patriarchal Religion: Principles of Ideological Critique of the Bible." *Journal for the Study of the Old Testament* 22 (1982): 54–66.

———. "The Subordination and Liberation of Women in Christian Theology: St. Paul and Sarah Grimké." *Soundings* 51 (1978): 168–81.

Russell, Letty. *The Liberating Word: A Guide to Non-Sexist Interpretation of the Bible*. Philadelphia: Westminster Press, 1976.

———, ed. *Feminist Interpretation of the Bible*. Philadelphia: Westminster Press, 1984.

Sakenfeld, Katherine Doob. "The Bible and Women: Bane or Blessing?" *Theology Today* 32 (October 1975): 222–33.

———. "Old Testament Perspectives: Methodological Issues." *Journal for the Study of the Old Testament* 22 (1982): 13–20.

Schottroff, Luise. "Women as Followers of Jesus in New Testament Times: An Exercise in Social-Historical Exegesis of the Bible." In *The Bible and Liberation: Political and Social Hermeneutics*, edited by Norman K. Gottwald, 418–27. Revised edition of *A Radical Religion Reader*. Maryknoll, N.Y.: Orbis Books, 1983.

Scroggs, Robin. "Paul and the Eschatological Woman." *Journal of the American Academy of Religion* 40 (September 1972): 283–303.

———. "Paul and the Eschatological Woman: Revisited." *Journal of the American Academy of Religion* 42 (September 1974): 532–37.

Smith, Derwood C. "Paul and the Non-Eschatological Woman " *Ohio Journal of Religious Studies* 4 (March 1976): 11–18.

Stendahl, Krister. *The Bible and the Role of Women: A Case Study in Hermeneutics*. Translated by Emilie T. Sander. Biblical Series 15, edited by John Reumann. Philadelphia: Fortress Press, 1966.

Swidler, Leonard. *Biblical Affirmations of Woman*. Philadelphia: Westminster Press, 1979.

———. "Jesus Was a Feminist." *Southeast Asia Journal of Theology* 13 (1971): 102–10.

Terrien, Samuel. "Toward a Biblical Theology of Womanhood." *Religion and Life* 42 (Autumn 1973): 322–33.

Tolbert, Mary Ann, ed. *The Bible and Feminist Hermeneutics*. Chico, Calif.: Scholars Press, 1983.

Trible, Phyllis. "Eve and Adam: Genesis 2–3 Re-read." In *Womanspirit Rising: A Feminist Reader in Religion*, edited by Carol Christ and Judith Plaskow, 74–83. San Francisco: Harper & Row, 1979.

———. "Feminist Hermeneutics and Biblical Study." *Christian Century* 99 (3–10 February 1982): 116–18.

———. *God and the Rhetoric of Sexuality*. Overtures to Biblical Theology 2. Philadelphia: Fortress Press, 1978.

———. "Good Tidings of Great Joy: Biblical Faith Without Sexism." *Christianity and Crisis* 34 (4 February 1974): 12–16.

———. *Texts of Terror: Literary-Feminist Readings of Biblical Narratives*. Overtures to Biblical Theology 13. Philadelphia: Fortress Press, 1984.

———. "Two Women in a Man's World: A Reading of the Book of Ruth."

Soundings 59 (Fall 1976): 251–79.

———. "Women in the Old Testament." *Interpreter's Dictionary of the Bible.* Supplementary volume, 963–66. Nashville: Abingdon Press, 1976.

CHAPTER 2

Church, F. Forrester. "Sex and Salvation in Tertullian." *Harvard Theological Review* 68 (April 1975): 83–101.

Clark, Elizabeth. *Jerome, Chrysostom and Friends: Essays and Translations.* Studies in Women and Religion, vol. 2. New York: Edwin Mellen Press, 1979.

Fiorenza, Elisabeth Schüssler. "Word, Spirit and Power: Women in Early Christian Communities." In *Women of Spirit: Female Leadership in the Jewish and Christian Traditions*, edited by Rosemary Radford Ruether and Eleanor McLaughlin, 30–70. New York: Simon & Schuster, 1979.

Gryson, Roger. *The Ministry of Women in the Early Church.* Collegeville, Minn.: Liturgical Press, 1976.

Hess, Hamilton. "Changing Forms of Ministry in the Early Church." In *Sexism and Church Law*, edited by James A. Corriden, 43–57. New York: Paulist Press, 1977.

Irvin, Dorothy. "The Ministry of Women in the Early Church: The Archaeological Evidence." *Duke Divinity Review* 45 (1980): 76–86.

Klawiter, Frederick C. "The Role of Martyrdom and Persecution in Developing the Priestly Authority of Women in Early Christianity: A Case Study of Montanism." *Church History* 49 (September 1980): 251–61.

Laporte, Jean. *The Role of Women in Early Christianity.* Studies in Women and Religion, vol. 7. New York: Edwin Mellen Press, 1982.

Munro, Winsome. "Patriarchy and Charismatic Community in 'Paul.'" In *Women and Religion: Papers of the Working Group on Women and Religion 1972–73*, rev. ed., edited by Judith Plaskow and Joan Arnold Romero, 189–98. Missoula, Mont.: American Academy of Religion and Scholars' Press, 1974.

Pagels, Elaine. *The Gnostic Gospels.* New York: Random House, 1979.

Patterson, Lloyd. "Women in the Early Church: A Problem of Perspective." In *Toward a New Theology of Ordination: Essays on the Ordination of Women*, edited by Marianne H. Micks, 23–41. Somerville, Mass.: Greeno, Hadden & Co., 1976.

Phipps, William. *Influential Theologians on Wo/Man.* Washington, D.C.: University Press of America, 1980.

———. "The Menstrual Taboo in the Judaeo-Christian Tradition." *Journal of Religion and Health* 19 (Winter 1980): 298–303.

Ruether, Rosemary Radford. "Misogynism and Virginal Feminism in the Fathers of the Church." In *Religion and Sexism: Images of Woman in the Jewish and Christian Traditions*, edited by Rosemary Radford Ruether, 150–83. New York: Simon & Schuster, 1974.

Sprong, John S. "Misogyny: A Pattern as Ancient as Life" and "Women: Less Than Free in Christ's Church." In *Into the Whirlwind: The Future of the Church*, 73–103. New York: Seabury, 1983.

Tavard, George. *Women in the Christian Tradition.* Notre Dame, Ind.: Univ. of Notre Dame Press, 1973.

Wilson-Kastner, Patricia, G. Ronald Kastner, Ann Millin, Rosemary Rader, and Jeremiah Reedy. *A Lost Tradition: Women Writers of the Early Church*. Washington, D.C.: University Press of America, 1981.

CHAPTER 3

Bradford, Clare. "Julian of Norwich and Margery Kempe." *Theology Today* 35 (July 1978): 153–58.

Brown, Raymond E., Karl P. Donfried, Joseph A. Fitzmeyer, and John Reumann, eds. *Mary in the New Testament: A Collaborative Essay by Protestant and Roman Catholic Scholars*. Philadelphia: Fortress Press; New York: Paulist Press, 1978.

Bynum, Caroline Walker. *Jesus as Mother: Studies in the Spirituality of the High Middle Ages*. Berkeley and Los Angeles: Univ. of California Press, 1982.

Clark, Elizabeth. "Ascetic Renunciation and Feminine Advancement: A Paradox of Late Ancient Christianity." *Anglican Theological Review* 63 (July 1981): 240–57.

————. "John of Chrysostom and the Subintroductae." *Church History* 46 (June 1977): 171–85.

Feldman, Laurie A. "St. Catherine of Siena: An Exploration of the Feminine and Mystic." *Anima* 4 (Spring 1978): 57–63.

Garrett, Clarke. "Women and Witches: Patterns of Analysis." *Signs: Journal of Women in Culture and Society* 3 (Winter 1977): 461–70.

Gies, Frances, and Joseph Gies. *Women in the Middle Ages*. New York: Barnes & Noble, 1978.

Institoris, Henricus, and James Sprenger. *Malleus Maleficarum*. Translated by Montague Summers. New York: B. Bloom, 1970.

King, Margaret L. "The Religious Retreat of Isotta Nogarola (1418–1466): Sexism and Its Consequences in the Fifteenth Century." *Signs: Journal of Women in Culture and Society* 3 (Summer 1978): 807–22.

Lucas, Angela M. *Women in the Middle Ages: Religion, Marriage and Letters*. New York; St. Martin's Press, 1983.

McLaughlin, Eleanor. "Equality of Souls, Inequality of Sexes: Woman in Medieval Theology." In *Religion and Sexism: Images of Woman in the Jewish and Christian Traditions*, edited by Rosemary Radford Ruether, 213–66. New York: Simon & Schuster, 1974.

————. "Women, Power and the Pursuit of Holiness in Medieval Christianity." In *Women of Spirit: Female Leadership in the Jewish and Christian Traditions*, edited by Rosemary Radford Ruether and Eleanor McLaughlin, 100–130. New York: Simon & Schuster, 1979.

Morris, Joan. *The Lady Was a Bishop: The History of Women with Clerical Ordination and the Jurisdiction of Bishops*. New York: Macmillan Co., 1973.

Power, Eileen. *Medieval Women*. Cambridge: At the University Press, 1975.

Ruether, Rosemary Radford. *Mary—The Feminine Face of the Church*. Philadelphia: Westminster Press, 1977.

————. "The Persecution of Witches: A Case of Ageism and Sexism?" *Christianity and Crisis* 34 (23 December 1974): 291–95.

Russell, Jeffrey. *History of Witchcraft*. London: Thames & Hudson, 1980.

Stuard, Susan M., ed. *Women in Medieval Society*. Philadelphia: Univ. of Pennsylvania Press, 1976.

Szarmach, Paul. *An Introduction to the Medieval Mystics of Europe*. Albany, N.Y.: State Univ. of New York Press, 1984.

Warner, Marina. *Alone of All Her Sex: The Myth and Cult of the Virgin Mary*. New York: Alfred A. Knopf, 1976.

Wemple, Suzanne F. "Contemplative Life: The Search for Feminine Autonomy in the Frankish Kingdom." *Anima* 6 (Spring 1980): 131–36.

Yoshioka, Barbara. "Whoring After Strange Gods: A Narrative of Women and Witches." *Radical Religion* 1 (Summer/Fall 1974): 6–11.

CHAPTER 4

Bainton, Roland H. *Women of the Reformation, from Spain to Scandinavia*. Minneapolis: Augsburg Pub. House, 1977.

———. *Women of the Reformation: In France and England*. Minneapolis: Augsburg Pub. House, 1973.

———. *Women of the Reformation: In Germany and Italy*. Minneapolis: Augsburg Pub. House, 1971.

Bratt, John. "Role and Status of Women in the Writings of John Calvin." In *Renaissance, Reformation, Resurgence*, edited by Peter DeKlerk, 1–17. Grand Rapids: Calvin Theological Seminary, 1976.

Chrisman, Miriam U. "Women and the Reformation in Strasbourg 1490–1530." *Archive for Reformation History* 63 (1972): 143–67.

DeBoer, Willis. "Calvin on the Role of Women." In *Exploring the Heritage of John Calvin*, edited by David Holwerda, 236–72. Grand Rapids: Baker Book House, 1976.

Douglass, Jane Dempsey. "Christian Freedom: What Calvin Learned at the School of Women." *Church History* 53 (June 1984): 155–73.

———. "Women and the Continental Reformation." In *Religion and Sexism: Images of Woman in the Jewish and Christian Traditions*, edited by Rosemary Radford Ruether, 292–318. New York: Simon & Schuster, 1974.

———. *Women, Freedom, and Calvin*. Philadelphia: Westminster Press, 1985.

Greaves, Richard L. "The Role of Women in Early English Nonconformity." *Church History* 52 (September 1983): 299–311.

Irwin, Joyce L. *Womanhood in Radical Protestantism 1525–1675*. Studies in Women and Religion, vol. 1. New York: Edwin Mellen Press, 1979.

Roelker, Nancy. "The Appeal of Calvinism to French Noblewomen in the Sixteenth Century." *Journal of Interdisciplinary History* 2 (Spring 1972): 391–418.

———. "The Role of Noblewomen in the French Reformation." *Archive for Reformation History* 63 (1972): 168–95.

Scharffenorth, Gerta. *Becoming Friends in Christ: The Relationship Between Man and Woman in Luther*. LWF Studies: Reports and Texts from the Department of Studies. Geneva: Lutheran World Federation, 1983.

Steinmetz, David C. "Theological Reflections on the Reformation and the Status of Women." *Duke Divinity Review* 41 (Fall 1976): 197–207.

Thomas, Keith. "Women and the Civil War Sects." In *Crisis in Europe 1560–1660*, edited by Trevor Aston, 317–40. New York: Basic Books, 1965.

CHAPTER 5

Benson, Mary Sumner. *Women in Eighteenth Century America*. New York: Columbia Univ. Press, 1935. Reprint. New York: A.M.S. Press, 1976.

Calvo, Janis. "Quaker Women Ministers in Nineteenth Century America." *Quaker History* 63 (Autumn 1974): 75–93.

Cowring, Cedric. "Sex and Preaching in the Great Awakening." *American Quarterly* 20 (Fall 1968): 624–44.

George, Carol V. R. "Anne Hutchinson and the Revolution Which Never Happened." In *Remember the Ladies: New Perspectives on Women in American History*, edited by Carol V. R. George, 13–37. Syracuse, N.Y.: Syracuse Univ. Press, 1975.

Holliday, Carl. *Women's Life in Colonial Days*. Boston: Cornhill Publishing Co., 1922. Reprint. Detroit: Gale Research Co., 1970.

Huber, Elaine C. "'A Woman Must Not Speak': Quaker Women in the English Left Wing." In *Women of Spirit: Female Leadership in the Jewish and Christian Traditions*, edited by Rosemary Radford Ruether and Eleanor McLaughlin, 154–203. New York: Simon & Schuster, 1979.

James, Janet Wilson, ed. *Women in American Religion*. Philadelphia: Univ. of Pennsylvania Press, 1980.

King, Anne. "Anne Hutchinson and Anne Bradstreet." *International Journal of Women's Studies* 1 (September/October 1978): 445–67.

Koehler, Lyle. "The Case of the American Jezebels: Anne Hutchinson and Female Agitation During the Years of Antinomian Turmoil, 1636–1640." In *Our Sisters: Women in American Life and Thought*, edited by Jean Friedman and William Shade, 52–75. Boston: Allyn & Bacon, 1976.

Kraditor, Aileen, ed. *Up From the Pedestal: Selected Writings in the History of American Feminism*. Chicago: Quadrangle Books, 1968.

Loewenberg, Bert J., and Ruth Bogin, eds. *Black Women in Nineteenth Century American Life*. University Park, Pa.: Pennsylvania State Univ. Press, 1976.

Lumpkin, William L. "The Role of Women in 18th Century Virginia Baptist Life." *Baptist History and Heritage* 8 (1973): 158–67.

Malmsheimer, Lonna A. "Daughters of Zion: New England Roots of American Feminism." *New England Quarterly* 50 (September 1977): 484–504.

Masson, Margaret. "The Typology of the Female as a Model for the Regenerate: Puritan Preaching 1690–1730." *Signs: Journal of Women in Culture and Society* 2 (Winter 1976): 304–15.

Norton, Mary Beth. "'My Resting Reaping Times': Sarah Osborn's Defense of Her 'Unfeminine' Activities, 1767." *Signs: Journal of Women in Culture and Society* 2 (Winter 1976): 515–29.

Porterfield, Amanda. *Feminine Spirituality in America*. Philadelphia: Temple Univ. Press, 1970.

Ruether, Rosemary Radford, and Rosemary Skinner Keller, eds. *Women and Religion in America*. Vol. 2, *The Colonial and Revolutionary Periods*. San Francisco: Harper & Row, 1983.

Ryan, Mary P. *Womanhood in America: From Colonial Times to the Present*. 3d ed. New York: Franklin Watts, 1983.

Smith, Page. *Daughters of the Promised Land: Women in American History*. Boston:

Little, Brown & Co., 1970.

Spruill, Julia. *Women's Life and Work in the Southern Colonies*. Chapel Hill, N.C.: Univ. of North Carolina Press, 1938. Reprint. New York: Norton & Co., 1972.

Stein, Stephen. "A Note on Anne Dutton, Eighteenth Century Evangelical." *Church History* 44 (December 1975): 485–91.

Ulrich, Laurel Thatcher. *Good Wives: Image and Reality in the Lives of Women in Northern New England 1650–1750*. New York: Alfred A. Knopf, 1982.

―――. "Vertuous Women Found: New England Ministerial Literature, 1668–1735." In *Women in American Religion*, edited by Janet Wilson James, 67–87. Philadelphia: Univ. of Pennsylvania Press, 1980.

Women in New Worlds: Historical Perspectives on the Wesleyan Tradition. Vol. 1, edited by Hilah F. Thomas and Rosemary Skinner Keller. Vol. 2, edited by Rosemary Skinner Keller, Louise L. Queen, and Hilah F. Thomas. Nashville: Abingdon Press, 1981, 1982.

CHAPTER 6

Bass, Dorothy. "Their Prodigious Influence: Women, Religion and Reform in Antebellum America." In *Women of Spirit: Female Leadership in the Jewish and Christian Traditions*, edited by Rosemary Radford Ruether and Eleanor McLaughlin, 280–300. New York: Simon & Schuster, 1979.

Beaver, R. Pierce. *American Protestant Women in World Mission: History of the First Feminist Movement in North America*. Rev. ed. Grand Rapids: Wm. B. Eerdmans, 1980.

Cott, Nancy. *The Bonds of Womanhood: Woman's Sphere in New England, 1780–1835*. New Haven, Conn.: Yale Univ. Press, 1977.

―――. "Young Women in the Second Great Awakening in New England." *Feminist Studies* 3 (1975): 15–29.

Douglas, Ann. *The Feminization of American Culture*. New York: Alfred A. Knopf, 1977.

Fishburn, Janet Forsythe. *The Fatherhood of God and the Victorian Family: The Social Gospel in America*. Philadelphia: Fortress Press, 1981.

Flexner, Eleanor. *Century of Struggle: The Women's Rights Movement in the United States*. Cambridge, Mass.: Belknap Press of Harvard Univ. Press, 1975.

Harris, Barbara. *Beyond Her Sphere: Women and the Professions in American History*. Westport, Conn.: Greenwood Press, 1978.

Harrison, Beverly W. "Early Feminists and the Clergy: A Case Study in the Dynamics of Secularization." *Review and Expositor* 72 (Winter 1975): 41–52.

Hersh, Blanche Glassman. *The Slavery of Sex: Feminist Abolitionists in America*. Urbana: Univ. of Illinois Press, 1978.

Melder, Keith E. *Beginnings of Sisterhood: The American Woman's Rights Movement 1800–1850*. Studies in the Life of Women, edited by Gerda Lerner. New York: Schocken Books, 1977.

―――. "Ladies Bountiful: Organized Women's Benevolence in Early Nineteenth Century America." *New York History* 48 (July 1967): 231–54.

Rossi, Alice S. *The Feminist Papers: From Adams to deBeauvoir*. New York: Bantam Books, 1974.

Ruether, Rosemary Radford, and Rosemary Skinner Keller, eds. *Women and Reli-*

gion in America. Vol. 1, *The Nineteenth Century*. San Francisco: Harper & Row, 1981.

Smith-Rosenberg, Carroll. "Beauty, the Beast and the Militant Woman: A Case Study in Sex Roles and Social Stress in Jacksonian America." *American Quarterly* 23 (October 1971): 562–84.

Welter, Barbara. "The Cult of True Womanhood, 1820–1860." In *Dimity Convictions: The American Woman in the Nineteenth Century*, 21–41. Athens, Ohio: Ohio Univ. Press, 1976.

———. "The Feminization of American Religion, 1800–1860." In *Dimity Convictions: The American Woman in the Nineteenth Century*, 83–102. Athens, Ohio: Ohio Univ. Press, 1976.

———. "She Hath Done What She Could: Protestant Women's Missionary Careers in Nineteenth Century America." In *Women in American Religion*, edited by Janet Wilson James, 111–25. Philadelphia: Univ. of Pennsylvania Press, 1980.

CHAPTER 7

Dayton, Donald W. "Evangelical Roots of Feminism." *The Covenant Quarterly* 34 (November 1976): 41–56.

Dayton, Donald W., and Lucille Sider Dayton. "Women as Preachers: Evangelical Precedents." *Christianity Today* 19 (23 May 1975): 4–7.

Dayton, Lucille Sider, and Donald W. Dayton. "'Your Daughters Shall Prophesy': Feminism in the Holiness Movement." *Methodist History* 14 (January 1976): 67–92.

Hardesty, Nancy A. "No Rights But Human Rights." *Perkins Journal* 35 (Fall 1981): 58–62.

———. *Women Called to Witness: Evangelical Feminism in the Nineteenth Century*. Nashville: Abingdon Press, 1984.

Hardesty, Nancy, Lucille Sider Dayton, and Donald W. Dayton. "Women in the Holiness Movement: Feminism in the Evangelical Tradition." In *Women of Spirit: Female Leadership in the Jewish and Christian Traditions*, edited by Rosemary Radford Ruether and Eleanor McLaughlin, 226–54. New York: Simon & Schuster, 1979.

Hill, Suzan E. "*The Woman's Bible*: Reformulating Tradition." *Radical Religion* 8 (1977): 23–30.

Huber, Elaine C. "They Weren't Prepared to Hear: A Closer Look at *The Woman's Bible*." *Andover Newton Quarterly* 16 (March 1976): 271–76.

Murdoch, Norman H. "Female History in the Thought and Work of Catherine Booth." *Church History* 53 (September 1984): 348–62.

Smylie, James. "*The Woman's Bible* and the Spiritual Crisis." *Soundings* 59 (Fall 1976): 305–28.

Study Guide to The Woman's Bible. Seattle: Coalition Task Force on Women and Religion, 1975.

The Woman's Bible. Part I, Comments on Genesis, Exodus, Leviticus, Numbers and Deuteronomy. Part II, Comments on the Old and New Testaments from Joshua to Revelation. New York: European Publishing Co., 1892, 1895. Reprint. New York: Arno Press, 1972.

CHAPTER 8

Baker, Joan. "Women in Utopia: The Nineteenth Century Experience." In *Utopias: The American Experience*, edited by Gairdner Moment and Otto Kraushaar, 56–71. Metuchen, N.J.: Scarecrow Press, 1980.

Bednarowski, Mary Farrell. "Outside the Mainstream: Women's Religion and Women Religious Leaders in Nineteenth Century America." *Journal of the American Academy of Religion* 48 (June 1980): 207–31.

Campbell, D'Ann. "Woman's Life in Utopia: The Shaker Experiment in Sexuality Reappraised 1810–1860." *New England Quarterly* 51 (March 1978): 23–38.

Ewens, Mary. "Removing the Veil: The Liberated American Nun." In *Women of Spirit: Female Leadership in the Jewish and Christian Traditions*, edited by Rosemary Radford Ruether and Eleanor McLaughlin, 256–78. New York: Simon & Schuster, 1979.

————. *The Role of the Nun in Nineteenth Century America*. New York: Arno Press, 1978.

Fox, Margery. "Protest in Piety: Christian Science Revisited." *International Journal of Women's Studies* 1 (July/August 1978): 401–16.

Kenneally, James. "Eve, Mary and the Historians: American Catholicism and Women." In *Women in American Religion*, edited by Janet Wilson James, 190–206. Philadelphia: Univ. of Pennsylvania Press, 1980.

Kern, Louis J. *An Ordered Love: Sex Roles and Sexuality in Victorian Utopias—the Shakers, the Mormons and the Oneida Community*. Chapel Hill, N.C.: Univ. of North Carolina Press, 1981.

Kolmer, Elizabeth. "Catholic Women Religious and Women's History: A Survey of the Literature." In *Women in American Religion*, edited by Janet Wilson James, 127–39. Philadelphia: Univ. of Pennsylvania Press, 1980.

Moore, R. Laurence. "Spiritualist Medium: A Study of Female Professionalism in Victorian America." *American Quarterly* 27 (May 1975): 200–221.

Muncy, Raymond Lee. *Sex and Marriage in Utopian Communities*. Bloomington, Ind.: Indiana Univ. Press, 1973.

Zikmund, Barbara Brown. "The Feminist Thrust of Sectarian Christianity." In *Women of Spirit: Female Leadership in the Jewish and Christian Traditions*, edited by Rosemary Radford Ruether and Eleanor McLaughlin, 206–24. New York: Simon & Schuster, 1979.

CHAPTER 9

Boyd, Lois A., and R. Douglas Brackenridge. *Presbyterian Women in America: Two Centuries of a Quest for Status*. Presbyterian Historical Society Contributions to the Study of Religion 9. Westport, Conn.: Greenwood Press, 1983.

Brereton, Virginia, and Christa Klein. "American Women in Ministry: A History of Protestant Beginning Points." In *Women in American Religion*, edited by Janet Wilson James, 171–90. Philadelphia: Univ. of Pennsylvania Press, 1980.

Carter, Norene, and Rosemary Radford Ruether. "Entering the Sanctuary: The Struggle for Priesthood in Contemporary Episcopalian and Roman Catholic Experience." In *Women of Spirit: Female Leadership in the Jewish and Christian Traditions*, edited by Rosemary Radford Ruether and Eleanor McLaughlin, 356–83. New York: Simon & Schuster, 1979.

Harrison, Beverly Wildung. "Sexism and the Contemporary Church: When Evasion Becomes Complicity." In *Sexist Religion and Women in the Church: No More Silence!*, edited by Alice Hageman, 195–216. New York: Association Press, 1974.

Mitchell, Norma. "From Social to Radical Feminism: A Survey of Emerging Diversity in Methodist Women's Organizations, 1869–1974." *Methodist History* 13 (April 1975): 21–44.

Orthodox Women: Their Role and Participation in the Orthodox Church. Report on the Consultation of Orthodox Women, 11–17 September 1976, Agapia, Romania. Agapia, Romania: World Council of Churches, Subunit on Women in Church and Society, 1976.

Parvey, Constance F., ed. *The Community of Men and Women in the Church: The Sheffield Report*. Philadelphia: Fortress Press, 1983.

Thompson, Betty. *A Chance to Change: Women and Men in the Church*. Philadelphia: Fortress Press, 1982.

CHAPTER 10

Berry, Wanda Warren. "Images of Sin and Salvation in Feminist Theology." *Anglican Theological Review* 60 (January 1978): 25–54.

Cahill, Lisa Sowle. *Between the Sexes: Foundations for a Christian Ethics of Sexuality*. Philadelphia: Fortress Press, 1985.

Carroll, Jackson, Barbara Hargrove, and Adair Lummis. *Women of the Cloth: New Opportunity for the Churches*. New York: Harper & Row, 1983.

Chittister, Joan. *Women, Ministry and the Church*. New York: Paulist Press, 1983.

Christ, Carol P. *Diving Deep and Surfacing: Women Writers on Spiritual Quest*. Boston: Beacon Press, 1978.

Christ, Carol P., and Judith Plaskow, eds. *Womanspirit Rising: A Feminist Reader in Religion*. San Francisco: Harper & Row, 1979.

Coll, Regina. *Women and Religion: A Reader for the Clergy*. New York: Paulist Press, 1982.

Collins, Sheila. *A Different Heaven and Earth: A Feminist Perspective on Religion*. Valley Forge, Pa.: Judson Press, 1974.

———. "Toward a Feminist Theology." *Christian Century* 89 (2 August 1972): 796–99.

Cornwall Collective. *Your Daughters Shall Prophesy: Feminist Alternatives in Theological Education*. New York: Pilgrim Press, 1980.

Daly, Mary. *Beyond God the Father: Toward a Philosophy of Women's Liberation*. Boston: Beacon Press, 1973.

———. *The Church and the Second Sex*. With a New Feminist Postchristian Introduction by the Author. New York: Harper Colophon Books, 1968, preface and introduction 1975.

———. *Gyn/Ecology: The Metaethics of Radical Feminism*. Boston: Beacon Press, 1978.

Ermath, Margaret Sittler. *Adam's Fractured Rib: Observations on Women in the Church*. Philadelphia: Fortress Press, 1970.

Fiorenza, Elisabeth Schüssler. "Feminist Theology as a Critical Theology of Liberation." *Theological Studies* 36 (December 1975): 605–26.

Goldenberg, Naomi B. *Changing of the Gods: Feminism and the End of Traditional*

Religions. Boston: Beacon Press, 1979.

Goldstein, Valerie Saiving. "The Human Situation: A Feminine View." *Journal of Religion* 40 (April 1960): 100–112.

Grant, Jacquelyn. "Black Women and the Church." In *All the Women Are White, All the Blacks Are Men, But Some of Us Are Brave*, edited by Gloria T. Hull, Patricia Bell Scott, and Barbara Smith, 141–52. Old Westbury, N.Y.: Feminist Press, 1982.

Gross, Rita M., ed. *Beyond Androcentrism: New Essays on Women and Religion.* Missoula, Mont.: Scholars Press, 1977.

Harkness, Georgia. *Women in Church and Society.* Nashville: Abingdon Press, 1972.

Hoover, Theressa. "Black Women and the Churches: Triple Jeopardy." In *Sexism and the Churches: No More Silence!*, edited by Alice Hageman, 63–76. New York: Association Press, 1974.

Jewett, Paul. *The Ordination of Women.* Grand Rapids: Wm. B. Eerdmans, 1980.

Lehman, Edward. "Organizational Resistance to Women in Ministry." *Sociological Analysis: A Journal in the Sociology of Religion* 42 (Summer 1981): 101–18.

McFague, Sallie. *Metaphorical Theology: Models of God in Religious Language.* Philadelphia: Fortress Press, 1982.

Micks, Marianne H. *Our Search for Identity: Humanity in the Image of God.* Philadelphia: Fortress Press, 1982.

Morton, Nelle. *The Journey Is Home.* Boston: Beacon Press, 1985.

Murray, Pauli. "Black Theology and Feminist Theology: A Comparative View." In *Black Theology: A Documentary History*, edited by Gayraud Wilmore and James H. Cone, 398–417. Maryknoll, N.Y.: Orbis Books, 1979.

Plaskow, Judith. *Sin, Sex and Grace: Women's Experience and the Theologies of Reinhold Niebuhr and Paul Tillich.* Washington, D.C.: University Press of America, 1980.

The Power of Language Among the People of God and the Language About God: "Opening the Door": A Resource Document. New York: United Presbyterian Church in the U.S.A., n.d.

Ruether, Rosemary Radford. "Crisis in Sex and Race: Black Theology vs. Feminist Theology." *Christianity and Crisis* 34 (15 April 1974): 67–73.

————. *New Woman/New Earth: Sexist Ideologies and Human Liberation.* New York: Seabury, 1975.

————. *Sexism and God-Talk: Toward a Feminist Theology.* Boston: Beacon Press, 1984.

————. *Womanguides: Readings Toward a Feminist Theology.* Boston: Beacon Press, 1985.

Russell, Letty. *Human Liberation in a Feminist Perspective: A Theology.* Philadelphia: Westminster Press, 1974.

————, ed. *Changing Contexts of Our Faith.* Philadelphia: Fortress Press, 1985.

Stone, Merlin. *When God Was a Woman.* New York: Harcourt Brace Jovanovich, 1976.

Washbourn, Penelope. "Authority or Idolatry?: Feminine Theology and the Church." *Christian Century* 92 (29 October 1975): 961–64.

Weidman, Judith, ed. *Women Ministers: How Women Are Redefining Traditional*

Roles. New York: Harper & Row, 1981.

Wilson-Kastner, Patricia. "Christianity and the New Feminist Religions." *Christian Century* 98 (9 September 1981): 864–68.

———. *Faith, Feminism and the Christ*. Philadelphia: Fortress Press, 1983.

"Women Clergy—How Their Presence Is Changing the Church: A Symposium by Five Women on the Seminary Campus." *Christian Century* 96 (7 February 1979): 122–28.

SUBJECT INDEX

SCRIPTURE INDEX